A THEOLOGY AS BIG AS THE CITY

RAY BAKKE

InterVarsity Press
Downers Grove, Illinois

InterVarsity Press® is the book-publishing division of InterVarsity Christian Fellowship®, a student movement active on campus at hundreds of universities, colleges and schools of nursing in the United States of America, and a member movement of the International Fellowship of Evangelical Students. For information about local and regional activities, write Public Relations Dept., InterVarsity Christian Fellowship, 6400 Schroeder Rd., P.O. Box 7895, Madison, WI 53707-7895.

Cover photograph: Richard Berenholtz/The Stock Market

ISBN 0-8308-1890-1

Printed in the United States of America ♾

Library of Congress Cataloging-in-Publication Data

Bakke, Raymond J., 1938-
    A theology as big as the city/Ray Bakke.
       p.   cm.
    Includes bibliographical references (p.   ).
    ISBN 0-8308-1890-1 (alk. paper)
    1. Cities and towns—Biblical teaching.   2. Cities and towns—
Religious aspects—Christianity.   3. City churches.   I. Title.
BS680.C5B35   1997
250'.9173'2—dc21
                                             96-29820
                                              CIP

21	20	19	18	17	16	15	14	13	12	11	10	9	8	7	6	5	4	3	2	1
14	13	12	11	10	09	08	07	06	05	04	03	02	01	00	99	98	97			

Dedication

In 1970, Hal Edwards of Christian Laity of Chicago and Bud Bylsma of Young Life met together in a "greasy-spoon" south-side restaurant and agreed they could best serve Christ and sustain their spirituality in this turbulent city if they did so with intentionality and accountability. Shortly thereafter, the late Bill Leslie, long-time pastor of LaSalle Street Church, with whom I was teaching Bible part time at Trinity College while we pastored neighboring churches, asked me if I would join their little group with the rather audacious title The Chicago Network. The group had two primary covenants: one to each other as friends, for the journey inward, and one to our city, Chicago, for the journey outward.

So, twenty-five years ago at a monthly meeting in the executive suite of Jim Beré, CEO of the Borg Warner Corporation, overlooking Michigan Avenue and Chicago's lakefront, the group laid hands on me in fervent prayer and I became part of the Network. Since that day we have met regularly to engage each other about the significance of biblical faith in Jesus Christ personally, vocationally and publicly in witness to Chicago and the world.

I cannot possibly describe the education I've received, the perspectives sharpened, the counsel given or solace shared as we have met almost monthly over the past quarter-century. These sisters and brothers have been there for me. To them, including Bill Leslie and Larry Davis, who are with the Lord, and to a few who, like Bud Bylsma, have moved on, I say thanks and dedicate this book.

Art Brown, *missionary and pastor, retired*
Delores Cross, *Chicago State University*
Hal Edwards, *Vision Quest*
Pete Hammond, *InterVarsity Christian Fellowship*
Bud Ipema, *Mid-America Leadership Foundation*
Herb Martin, *Progressive Community Church*
Janet Morrow, *Chicago civic leader, former director of* TRUST, *Inc.*
Gordon Murphy, *The* STOREHOUSE *of Vision Chicago*
Jan Niemeyer, *chaplain, Jonquil Hotel*
Bud Ogle, *Good News Partners*
Margaret Palmer, *Chicago civic leader, lawyer, former legislative assistant*
Don Wagner, *Evangelicals for Middle East Understanding*
Al Ward, *Communities in Schools*

Acknowledgments

I have an incredibly gifted young staff at International Urban Associates at 5151 North Clark Street in Chicago. Without them I could not be out of this city in ministry 200 or more days a year, much less try to write a book at the same time.

Andrea Faugerstrom, herself a theological seminary graduate, manages this office, and I can say without fear of contradiction that without her this book could never have been finished. She was all over the manuscript several times in recent months, as was Roger Johnson, IUA's researcher and newsletter editor.

Scott Bakke, my nephew, joined the IUA staff this year to organize my several-thousand-volume library in our new office location, among other projects. The truth is, Scott knows much better than I do where all my books are these days, and I have relied very heavily on him to pull together the references and bibliography for this manuscript.

The teamwork of our other colleagues, Lenore Knight and Elizabeth Lezark, and two former staff members, Lisa Tomkins-Rivera and Brian McLaughlin, who were with us during the writing of the first draft, enabled us to keep up with some forty-seven ministry events on five continents simultaneously with this book's emergence—even with the birth of Elizabeth's baby Katie in June!

Without them, and without my ever-appreciative and appreciated wife, Corean, this could not have been achieved.

As they've heard me say to so many others over the years, "My thanks and God's peace."

Introduction

Even now, forty years after first arriving in Chicago as a student, I am surprised that God would call me, the child of loggers and farmers, to ministry service in the largest cities of the world. The journey on which God has taken me, from rural Washington to inner-city Chicago to urban places around the world, is truly one of God's great miracles in my life.

This book is not primarily a text about cities or even about the theology of city in an abstract sense; it is about the map God used to get me into the city for life and work. I've discovered in recent years that people are much more interested in how I learn than in what I know. "How do you get there from here?" That is the question this book addresses.

Environments are never neutral. The city has been the context where my theology and ministry have been shaped. So, of necessity, descriptions of urban realities will weave their way throughout this text. But my central goal is to describe my personal quest to find a theology "as big as the city."

I want to show the process of transformational thinking and acting that occurred along the way to developing a worldview that seeks biblical integrity and spiritual faithfulness. I want to tell stories about the people, books and events—many from my early days of ministry—that helped revolutionize my theology of the city. As a result, this book will not address all of the most up-to-date dialogues in urban theology. I will trust you to accept that I've not quit reading to shape, critique and fill in the details of my theology.

My hope is that my stories will encourage the next generation of pastors, missionaries and agency directors to join me on this journey of learning what God has to say about the nature and mission of the church in a rapidly urbanizing world—and to take this journey with biblical integrity and faithfulness to the Holy Spirit's leading of the church throughout the nearly two thousand years since Pentecost.

The Urban Challenge

The spectacular growth of large cities on this planet represents an awesome challenge to the church of Jesus Christ on all six continents. In 1900, 8 percent of the world's population lived in cities. By the year 2000, that number will be nearly 50 percent.

Moreover, if we consider the impact of *urbanization* and *urbanism* in our world, we can see that city growth is even more significant. By *urbanization* we mean the development of cities as *places* where size, density and heterogeneity are measured. We might call this the *magnet* function of cities, drawing humanity into huge metroplexes. By *urbanism* we mean the development of city as *process*—that is, the *magnifier* function of cities, spinning out urban values, products and lifestyles into a world linked by media, even in rural and small-town places.

You see, there is no place to hide. The city is a media stage prop in this cybernetic era, and its presence will impact everyone eventually. So, even in places far from large cities, banks, businesses and families are linked up to urban centers. We must acknowledge, then, that not only do nearly three billion of the earth's nearly six billion persons live in cities, the other three billion are being urbanized as well. Sorry, you have an urban future, whether you like it or not.

The Challenge of Numbers

The challenge we face as we approach the twenty-first century is *demographic* or numerical. We will add one billion people to the planet in the next ten years, mostly in Asia and mostly in cities. That's significant because the world is Asianizing as fast as it is urbanizing. These twin realities, like engines on a Boeing 777, drive the planet away from the Atlantic-centered world and toward the Pacific-Rim century. It's a trend we've known for five hundred years.

The Challenge of Migration
The challenge is also *missiological*. As we move away from a world of nations to a world of interconnected multinational cities, it's clear that the frontier of mission has shifted. The majority of the world's non-Christians will not be geographically distant peoples, but culturally distant peoples who often reside together within the shadows of urban spires in the metro areas of every continent (except Antarctica, of course). Mission is no longer about crossing the oceans, jungles and deserts, but about crossing the streets of the world's cities. From now on, nearly all ministry will be crosscultural amid the urban pluralism caused by the greatest migration in human history from Southern hemispheres to the North, from East to West and, above all, from rural to urban.

The Challenge of Church Structure
Of course, the challenge is also *ecclesiastical*, for every church and denomination will face the reality that while the church may keep the same basic functions (worship, evangelism, discipleship, stewardship, fellowship and service), the forms they take must adapt to the pluralized and kaleidoscopic realities of a twenty-four-hour city. Like supermarkets, hospitals and police departments, churches will require day pastors and night pastors for twenty-four-hour environments in all languages, cultures and class groups, now residing in the same communities. That will be a stretch for pastors, but also for the seminaries and training institutions that have served churches in the past by providing leadership for them.

The Challenge of Funding

Moreover, this challenge is *financial*. We've sold mission in the past on a scale that fits comfortably with rural and small-town environments where "the bang for the buck" is visible and cost-effective. Urban mission, on the other hand, is financially threatening because of escalating human need and the failure of other social institutions to carry their share of the costs. Hospitals and health-care delivery systems in U.S. cities may finally be sicker than the patients in their wards. In fact, for many the church is the only institution that still has presence and credibility. The costs are enormous, and the discretionary income of average congregations is marginal. How shall we address this challenge?

We Need an Urban Theology

As formidable as these and other challenges may be, it is the thesis of this book that the primary challenge is *theological*. Most Christians still read the Bible through rural lenses. Furthermore, the evangelical church seems to be retreating even further from seeing our God as One who engages external-world reality to seeing only One who meets our personal needs and solves our personal problems.

Yet the Bible clearly describes a God who is completely interested and involved with both the structures and the individuals that compose society. The schism in the church that has pitted social and personal ministries against each other in the city, a tragic legacy of the fundamentalist-modernist controversy early in the twentieth century, still marginalizes the church's ministry in the rapidly urbanizing developing world. The church must learn how to go up to the urban powerful and down to the urban powerless with equal integrity.

Greater theologians than I have contributed much to my thinking over the years. Years ago, when our cities were exploding around us, Gabriel Fackre suggested that there are two benefits of revolutions: they help us become informed, and they help us define our priorities. That's exactly what happened to me. This book is the product of that journey. In 1966 I began to read the Bible with urban eyes. I looked at the 1,250 uses of the word *city* in Scripture and developed case studies on cities and persons who lived in cities. Then, because I taught church history at McCormick Seminary in Chicago from 1969 to 1977 while pastoring an inner-city church, I had the wonderful opportunity to study and preach the texts of both testaments and try to make sense of them for a largely unlettered congregation in a public-aid and mixed-racial context. I likened it to Moses' experience of pastoring a largely unemployed community of mud-brick-making migrants in a bad neighborhood for forty years on "food stamps" called manna.

Since I am a self-described "historical charismatic"—one who believes that the Holy Spirit has been teaching the church for nearly two thousand years—I cannot talk about a theology of the city without reference to the many choice servants throughout history whose footprints I have followed into the city and from whose successes and failures I continue to learn. You will meet some of these people in the chapter entitled "Urban Family Album."

In recent years I've been able to share Bible studies with urban church leaders, both lay and clergy, in over two hundred of the world's largest cities. It's my greatest privilege. Lectures on urban sociology and mission strategy get warm receptions, but the greatest enthusiasm by far comes from those pastors who are trying to find God's Word for embattled followers of Jesus on the front lines of cities. From them, as from my urban congregations earlier, I've learned so much. And for them this book is written during Epiphany (witness season) of 1996.

1
A JOURNEY
TO THE CITY

He led them by a straight way
to a city where they could settle.
Psalm 107:7

SAXON, WASHINGTON, IS A FARMING and logging community about a hundred miles north of Seattle and seventy-five miles southeast of Vancouver, Canada. The South Fork of the Nooksack River emerges from the Twin Sisters Mountains in the Cascade range, dominated by nearby Mount Baker, which looms like a giant ice-cream cone over the valley. Images of Switzerland come to mind.[1]

The natural beauty of this place belies the economic struggles and hard times of the families that lived there, including my own. The valley of sturdy Scandinavians lived modestly without great expectations. After World War II, when I was a child, the logging, dairy and fishing industries were in transition. Incomes required more than one job per family plus children's summer employment on the farms. Civilization was remote. Montana was considered "out east." The newspaper came by mail a day late. Life was organized around the local high school and its programs in those days before television. In the words of comedian Dick Gregory, "We was broke, but not po'."

Lutheran pietism pervaded the culture of our valley. The little Lutheran church, which survived until I was twelve years old, stood across the road from the cemetery, which we all knew was the "Alumni Association" of our little church. Half of my family was in the church; the other half was in the cemetery.

Dedicated to God

Before each of his kids was born, Dad took a walk into the woods and dedicated us to God—a fact he didn't tell us until years later. Since there were only a few of us boys in the little church who were about the same age, we kept the same Sunday-school teacher, a Swedish logger named Roy Johnson, for ten years until high-school graduation. In fact, when the church closed its doors for lack of denominational support, we adjourned to Roy and Gladys's house in nearby Acme and continued as a community Sunday school.

When I was a teenager our Sunday-school class studied what the Bible taught about baptism, and several of us were baptized by a lay preacher. Since we never had a pastor at our church, I had no idea what pastors did. We did have missionaries come through on occasion and show slides; I thought God might be calling me to missions.

Meanwhile, I was asking everyone for counsel about the future. I grew up hoping to be a history teacher and football coach, because those were the best of the models available as I saw it. A friend of my Sunday-school teacher thought I should spend a year in Bible training and then go on to prepare for teaching or coaching. He suggested I consider Moody Bible Institute in Chicago. I had never heard of the school, but it sounded like a way out of the valley. I applied late and was accepted on probation. My cousin Gordon was also accepted, so we traveled together on a Greyhound bus with a box of precooked fried chicken and a three-day supply of food to Chicago for study in the big city.

A Bridge to the Twentieth-Century City

Moody was a bridge into the twentieth century for me. It was at the heart of the city geographically and, in those years, amazingly open to it culturally. I joined the choir and toured the U.S., Canada and much of Western Europe in a three-year period.

Meanwhile, Corean, the young woman who was to become my wife, left her small town in the Ozarks to come to Moody to study music. For many years she had been the only student in her grade level at their one-room school. We met when we were both assigned to the same ministry team at a skid-row mission.

Corean was rejecting the Southern culture of racism, and in 1957 she sought an African-American roommate, Anita Jefferson. Anita, a singer and pastor's wife, remains a significant family friend to this day.

In 1959, after finishing my studies at Moody, I began ministry as an assistant pastor back in Seattle with responsibilities for youth and music, directing three choirs and three youth groups while attending Seattle Pacific College (now Seattle Pacific University). Early that year a tenor in my adult choir gave me a copy of Martin Luther King's *Stride Toward Freedom,* and I knew immediately that if I were an urban pastor I'd doubtless be a white among blacks. I needed to confront my own racism, naiveté and ignorance.[2] I would need to sort and sift my own culture and its values.

The City and Human Identity

The following year, in 1960, John Kennedy, a Roman Catholic, was elected president. His vice president, Lyndon Johnson, a Southern Protestant, had agreed to run and deliver the Southern vote in exchange for government reallocation of military and space funds. NASA went to Houston, and the biggest competitive defense contract ever awarded to Boeing in Seattle was rescinded by the new Secretary of Defense, Robert McNamara, and reallocated to Southern aerospace contractors. Almost overnight Seattle was unemployed. My growing congregation of blue-collar Boeing mechanics was laid off, jobless. Employed they were merely the extensions of the tools they used, and now they were discarded by their company.

In a rural area, when you ask people who they are, they usually describe their family and geography. But in a city, when asked who they are, people describe their vocation: "I'm a teacher," or "I work at the gas company." Clearly urban unemployment is more than an economic issue; it's an identity crisis. As a pastor, I was unprepared for the despair and hopelessness of my people. I realized then that cities are not places of random population statistics. Cities package people. A political decision made 3,000 miles away to shift capital to Texas and California had disemployed my congregation in Seattle. I knew I had to learn more about cities and their functions.

During this time my college studies in history, philosophy and political science were also pushing the boundaries of my cognitive map and forcing me to integrate my faith with what I was learning.

Meanwhile, our senior pastor left, and at age twenty-three I inherited a two-year interim pastorate of a church with more than 300 members.

One day a friend shared with me a rather dusty and dry biography of Charles Simeon, a nineteenth-century Anglican pastor from Cambridge (1759-1836). God used this book, *Charles Simeon,* by H. C. G. Moule (written in 1892 and republished by InterVarsity Press in 1956), to redirect my life.[3] Simeon visited and preached to the poor of the city, loved scholarship and lived at a college in Cambridge, mentored pastors, inspired his ministry assistants (curates) to consider overseas missions, appointed chaplains for prison ships to Australia, and met for fifty years with Wilberforce, Pitt, Venn, Moore and others at Clapham in London to help England's Parliament pass the laws to ban slavery in 1807 and 1837.

For the first time in my life I saw what an urban church and its pastor could be and do if they combined biblical and theological integrity with contextual engagement of the issues of the day. I adopted the Anglican Simeon as my Baptist pastoral model and made plans to pursue both seminary and graduate studies. I was twenty-three when I read the book; Simeon was twenty-three when he became the pastor at Holy Trinity Cambridge.

Corean and I married in 1960 and soon had two remarkably large, robust boys. Our third child, our daughter, was seriously damaged by rubella in early pregnancy and was dead at birth on April 21, 1965. While presiding at her funeral in our little country cemetery, with mixed feelings I announced to the hundred or so family members and friends gathered there that we would be moving to Chicago to attend seminary but leaving our daughter there with them. For nearly nine months we'd grappled with the serious issues of a brain-, heart- and eye-damaged child. We had no insurance, and I was a month away from college graduation. I prayed knowing I'd probably have to give up seminary and get a job to pay for an institutionalized child. I've often wondered how to thank a little girl for giving her life so that I could be a pastor.

Explosions of the Sixties

Chicago in 1965 was anything but a happy city. Our Edgewater-Uptown community, about one by one-and-a-quarter miles, contained 60,000 people. We soon learned more than sixty nations had representatives in the local high school, which was teaching in eleven languages. Finding that more than 25 percent of all the nations of the world now lived in my community forced me to ask yet another question: *Why is the whole world coming to Chicago, and how does God feel about this?*

Chicago, like Newark, Los Angeles, Detroit and other cities, exploded in riots in the early sixties. I read *The Secular City*, by Harvey Cox, when it was first published in 1965.[4] While it was wonderfully informative, it was far too optimistic for the city I was experiencing. Not only was my city on fire, but the evangelicals I knew were fleeing the city in droves. It was called the "white fright, white flight" syndrome. These were my people, the ones who had the "right view" of inspired, inerrant Scriptures, the "right view" of missions—the ones who believed "greater is he that is in you than he that is in the world." They fled!

Nothing prepared me for the cultural captivity and failure of my church under pressure. If Christianity was not a game, if God's agenda was to empty the cities of Christian believers, then I assumed no sociological rationale should keep me there either, especially when my family was at risk. I had to have some answers. I was enrolled at Trinity Evangelical Divinity School in the northern suburbs of Chicago, but we lived in the inner city near the church where I was a ministry assistant.

On November 16, 1965, after studying late for a seminary class, I went downstairs in our apartment to turn down the thermostat for the night. I smelled gas and noticed the stove pilot light was out. I opened the back door to let the gas dissipate, lit a match from the box on the refrigerator, and in a flash blew up the building. The flames went fifty feet out into the alley, and the explosion blew out forty-five windows.

Still conscious, I dove into a bathroom and put out the fire in my hair, screamed for Corean to evacuate, fled to the alley and was driven to the emergency room of the nearby university hospital. Two doctors talked to me while they worked on me in order to keep me from going into shock. On my left a Chinese woman physician described how she had fled from China to Korea to Chicago. "This is the Promised Land," she said as she clipped charred skin from my left arm, hand and face.

Meanwhile, the doctor on my right side was a Cuban refugee. He had owned two hospitals in Cuba but had given them to Castro to buy five tickets for his family so they could come to Chicago. "Yes," he said, "this is the Promised Land."

Well, here I was, God's newly arrived urban minister, seminary student, father and assistant pastor of a nearby Baptist church. I had come to serve, but now I was helpless and being served by refugees from China and Cuba, one yellow and one brown. God was teaching me lessons outside the normal seminary curriculum.

Can Evangelicals Survive in the City?

An uncle transported our kids back to Seattle, where they stayed during my recovery, and Corean went to class for me at the seminary. We survived, but we were much in debt financially after having just buried our daughter, and we were living 2,000 miles from family in a turbulent inner city. But the greatest crisis I faced was theological. I didn't have a theology that addressed the world I was experiencing. My theology was not adequate for the issues I was facing in ministry or in my family.

Then in January 1966, while reading a plethora of urban litera-ture, I was provoked by a Chicago writer's article with the title "Why Evangelicals Can't Survive in the City."[5] In essence, the author suggested that the Bible is a very rural book about a very rural God who makes gardens and whose favorite people are shepherds and vine growers, and whose least favorite folks are urban dwellers. Consider David, God's favorite. As long as he stayed on the farm, played with sheep and wrote songs, he was okay. When he moved into Jerusalem, he got all messed up in politics. The lesson: Stay away from Jerusalem. Stay away from Chicago. This author ob-served that conservative Christians who devour Scripture as God's inerrant Word swallow this antiurban bias. Without knowing it, their values are skewed in an anticity direction. To walk with God eventually requires a departure from the city.

Like reading about Charles Simeon, reading this essay challenged me in the midst of the turbulence of my city. As I was reading, I was watching the flight of my church to the suburbs. Was he right? Is the Bible a rural book and the God of the Bible a rural God? Obviously, I had to know for myself. I vowed to commit to a new, focused Scripture study—one which, in fact, has taken the rest of my life.

I also realized that I didn't love Chicago, because I didn't yet know it. Corean and I decided that I would drop out of Trinity Seminary for a year but continue in my part-time ministry. Corean would have the opportunity to go to school while I pursued two new agendas: first, to get my head and heart around Chicago; and second, to see if there is a theology for the city in the Bible. A good revolution will do two things: free you to become informed, and define your priorities.

Theologian Karl Barth is famous for his observation that the Bible should be read hand in hand with the newspaper. I modified this advice to reading the Bible while spending an entire year visiting Chicago's seventy-seven inner-city communities. My vantage point, the lens through which I read Scripture, became the inner city, which one colleague has called "Third-World USA."

After a year of immersion in the city and the Scriptures, I returned to Trinity highly motivated, knowing exactly what I needed to study. I may have the record for the most independent study courses and waived requirements, for which I remain profoundly grateful. I loaded up on Bible and church history courses, which required contextual analysis in search of transferable concepts. I discovered I learn best by analogy. Ironically, the least practical courses for me were the so-called practical theology courses, where professors were prescriptive with a "here's-how-you-do-it" mentality. Early on I realized most of these courses presupposed a social location for the church that was off my urban map.

I had many superb courses at Trinity in those very "yeasty" years, but it was hard to concentrate on reading in a library when Martin Luther King and Bobby Kennedy were being killed and our cities were exploding. The late Paul Little came to Trinity from InterVarsity to teach evangelism, which he modeled by taking his students to university campuses to critique and learn from his approach. A group of us "embryonic urbanites" approached Paul and asked him to teach us a course in urban evangelism. He confessed he didn't know anything about it and said we should engage in it and teach him. This turned out to be a life- and ministry-transforming course for several of us. Here was the academic reversal: the vulnerable professor as learner, encourager and interpreter. We, the students, organized the course and dragged Paul all over Chicago for ten weeks of exciting learning as a student community. For Paul Little, Jesus was clearly more than a message; his itinerancy with a band of disciples was a model. I've made it a norm to teach this way. It's not efficient, but it has been very effective. Obviously, teaching is much more than mere course content.

Seeking the Peace of Chicago

At this time we had two boys approaching school age. How we would educate them became an important issue. I remember meditating on a chapter in Jeremiah one day. The Jerusalem exiles were told:

This is what the LORD Almighty, the God of Israel, says to all those I carried into exile from Jerusalem to Babylon: "Build houses and settle down; plant gardens and eat what they produce. Marry and have sons and daughters; find wives for your sons and give your daughters in marriage, so that they too may have sons and daughters. Increase in number there; do not decrease. Also, seek the peace and prosperity of the city to which I have carried you into exile. Pray to the LORD for it, because if it prospers, you too will prosper." Yes, this is what the LORD Almighty, the God of Israel, says: "Do not let the prophets and diviners among you deceive you. Do not listen to the dreams you encourage them to have. They are prophesying lies to you in my name. I have not sent them," declares the LORD.

This is what the LORD says: "When seventy years are completed for Babylon, I will come to you and fulfill my gracious promise to bring you back to this place. For I know the plans I have for you," declares the LORD, "plans to prosper you and not to harm you, plans to give you hope and a future." (Jer 29:4-11)

The straightforward logic of this text gripped me. First, these refugees were not victims as they had thought. They were on a mission sent by God to the enemy city (v. 4). Second, they were to raise their kids there (v. 6); third, they were to seek the *shalom* or just peace of the city Babylon (v. 7); and finally, God would retrieve them in due time (v. 11). Logically, if Jewish refugees in Babylon could unpack their suitcases, raise their children and seek the *shalom* of Babylon, how much more could we be expected to do this in Chicago and be blessed of God. We chose to stay and raise our children in inner-city public schools.

A friend introduced me to a professional football player with a special call to reach street kids. Jim Queen and I began a journey that resulted in the founding of Inner-city Athletic Mission to work with some rather violent gangs. One weekend thirty members of a gang committed their lives to follow Jesus! We took them to nearby churches, where they experienced some joy initially, then discomfort resulting in discrimination later. One by one the kids left the churches. I had a lot to learn about the nature, mission and realities of urban congregations. Issues of class and race, especially among the ethnic churches I knew best, raised another set of issues for theology and pastoral ministry.

Moses, My Pastoral Mentor
In 1969 I became pastor of a small inner-city church which ultimately birthed several Spanish daughter churches and a Spanish language seminary. The new people in the parish were immigrants and migrants. Most of them were poor and had non-English-speaking backgrounds.

Moses became my mentor. Brilliantly educated ("in all the wisdom of the Egyptians," according to Stephen in Acts 7:22), with a postgraduate internship in the desert, he was called of God to lead a mud-brick-making migrant group into the worst neighborhood of the Middle East, where they were largely unemployed for forty years. How Moses did human and community development that integrated spiritual values intrigued me then (and still does) as a pastoral model.

During this time I also began teaching and studying at McCormick Theological Seminary in Chicago. This Presbyterian seminary hosted the Presbyterian Institute for Industrial Relations Library, which I desired to access in order to be in dialogue with the World and National Councils of Churches' urban and rural mission experiences. I spent an entire year studying Roger Williams's conflict with John Cotton and other Massachusetts Puritans over the treatment of indigenous Indians. As Perry Miller's research brilliantly showed, Williams, who launched the American Baptist movement in Providence in 1639, could never accept their allegorical interpretation of Scripture, seeing New England as New Canaan and the Indians as the Amalekites or Canaanites to be banished from the land.[6]

These were highly stimulating years, working on cutting-edge urban issues framed historically but in the context of the radically explosive civil rights and Vietnam eras. One experience summarizes it. The pastor of First Presbyterian Church in Woodlawn, Rev. John Fry, had become famous nationally, because the FBI had raided his church when they heard John had negotiated a gang truce involving the Blackstone Rangers and had their guns stored in the church safe.

In the wild late sixties, you could not imagine a more admired pastor on our campus—a classic Princeton Seminary grad, former Marine, now the epitome of an antiestablishment prourban pastor. One day in the lunchroom a student asked John what it took to be a really "with it" pastor. He replied, "Unless you can read Hebrew without the vowel points and translate any passage in the Greek New Testament inside fifteen minutes, you have no business in the ministry." He paused for a moment while the students went into shock, then continued, "Because if you can't tell me where the church has been, you have no business telling me where it ought to go." I have never forgotten those words.[7]

This principle seems clear: the further one goes into the avant-garde frontier of creative ministry, the more important it becomes that we be deeply rooted in the biblical, theological and historical tradition. We need deep roots to survive in urban ministry.

The Global Urban World

In my continued studies of global urban migration, I was forced to confront the greatest migration in human history; the southern hemisphere coming north, and the east coming west, and *everyone* coming to the cities. The urban literature of rage, injustice and black-and-white issues did not address the global realities. That lens was too small. The largest cities of the world do not have black-white problems; they are yellow and brown respectively (Tokyo, Mexico City and so on).

On the other hand, the missiological literature was generally informed by tribal anthropology rather than urban sociology, so it didn't touch the issues I was facing, except by analogy. For so long, missions had represented the white man's burden, a Victorian "end run" around the cities of America and Europe to convert the jungle peoples of the world. Urban blacks especially expressed antimission feelings. I understood much better when, as usual, I encountered the issue historically. In 1890 David Livingstone's colleague Henry M. Stanley wrote his classic, *In Darkest Africa: The Way In*. In response, William Booth, the founder of the Salvation Army, shortly thereafter produced his classic, *In Darkest England: The Way Out*.[8]

Clearly I had to read the literature of both streams to understand the urban mission of God's church worldwide, for both the urban parish literature and the mission literature from post-World War II on suffered from a similar parochialism.

In 1971 Billy Graham held an evangelistic crusade in Chicago while the Vietnam protests against Richard Nixon were permeating the city. Television was making an enormous impact on the practice of mass evangelism, forcing me to reflect on John 1:14, "The Word became flesh and made his dwelling among us." In the name of this incarnate Jesus Christ, it appeared we now were implementing media strategies to save the city from which the church was physically withdrawing. I thought of the Vietnam War, where we parked our B52s on Guam, flew at 37,000 feet, bombed the Vietnamese and returned for our night's sleep while we pulled out the ground troops. It didn't work, of course. We lost the war. Our technologically advanced strategies did not work. Cities are far too complex a matrix to yield to ministry from a safe distance through the media. All this forced me to ask myself, *Is Jesus just our message or is he also our model?* In fact, we know now that nearly all urban persons come to Christ through relationships, not through media. The bigger the city, the higher this percentage seems to be.

Eight years later, in 1979, the Lausanne Committee for World Evangelization, begun by Billy Graham and chaired at that time by his gifted and irenic brother-in-law, evangelist Leighton Ford, asked me to serve as a large city consultant, in which role I held consultations in more than two hundred cities on six continents. At first, I thought that if pastors had good information and motivation, they could bring renewal to city churches and transform persons and places. I was wrong. By 1989 it was clear to me after "quick and dirty" surveys in some fifty cities (just Second- and Third-World) that 85 to 90 percent of all major barriers to effective urban ministry are not in our cities at all—they are inside our churches. Besides informing and motivating, our urban consultations had to deal with the real issues of intimidation in pastors and congregations in cities as different as Cairo, Chicago and Copenhagen.

Now as we look at cities in the nineties in North America and elsewhere, we face five new urban realities: a crack cocaine epidemic, assault weapons, massive numbers of homeless children, HIV-AIDS, and what *Time* magazine has called "the browning of America." Jonathan Kozol has written yet another volume[9] to remind us that children are suffering and dying in our cities. The elderly—now the fastest-growing group in society—seem to be getting in the way. The needs of the urban population are greater than ever.

Jesus doubtless understands this great need, because he confronted it (see Mk 5:21-43, for example). As our cities swell with immigrants and migrants, I'm reminded that Jesus was born in a borrowed barn in Asia and became an African refugee in Egypt. So the Christmas story is about an international migrant. Furthermore, a whole villageful of baby boys died for Jesus before he had the opportunity to die for them on the cross. Surely this Jesus understands the pain of children who die for the sins of adults in our cities.

Theological Reflection

What follows is not exhaustive Bible study, though that important task certainly tempts me. Rather, what follows is a way of looking at often familiar texts from my own vantage point as an urban Christian and minister.

I think generally there are three ways to study the Bible. The first is simply to read and obey its commands. The second is to read and follow its examples, often learning by analogy, because while the Bible was written *for* us, it was written long ago *to* someone else. Those two worlds are often very different. Rich Bible study tools help bridge the chasm between the ancient world of the Scriptures and the near-twenty-first century of our times.

The third way of doing Bible study is to bring theological reflection to the text in the light of our own unique traditions and social context. When Joseph told his brothers, "You intended to harm me, but God intended it for good" (Gen 50:20), that is theological reflection. Mordecai does the same thing in Esther 4:14: "And who knows but that . . ." His reflection couldn't be dogmatic—in fact, God's name isn't even mentioned in the book. Yet he was attempting to understand what God had to do with his world.

For me the Bible has to confront the why questions and all the issues of urban life. My faith truly seeks understanding. How shall we read the world? Why did my baby die? (I know how, but why?) Where can I find an environmental theology to confront a toxic planet? How shall we reflect on the ever-widening gap between the "haves" and the "have-nots"? What is the relationship between the Christian faith and other faiths? What about the increasingly prevalent issue of sexual identity? What texts, themes or stories address these and other issues?

In 1974 I gave a lecture entitled "A Biblical Theology for Urban Ministry" at McCormick Theological Seminary in the afternoon and Moody Bible Institute at night. Moody and McCormick were once nearly sister schools, funded by the same people for different purposes, but by this time they represented diverse theological camps. Yet at both schools I encountered people whose preconceived ideas and beliefs put boundaries around certain biblical texts so they could affirm it as the Word of God but deny that it had any application to them.

Harvard scholar Henry Cadbury wrote a helpful book called *The Perils of Modernizing Jesus,* which warned against twisting the biblical text to fit our own issues or reconstructing God and Jesus in our own image.[10] This happens all too often in weekly sermons. But that's not what this book is about. Rather, this book simply describes the search made by an urban pilgrim to find a theology as big as the city in which I live and serve my Lord.

2
GOD'S HANDS ARE
IN THE MUD

In the beginning God created the heavens and the earth.
Now the earth was formless and empty,
darkness was over the surface of the deep,
and the Spirit of God was hovering over the waters.
Genesis 1:1-2

The LORD God formed the man from the dust of the ground
and breathed into his nostrils the breath of life,
and the man became a living being.

Now the LORD God had planted a garden in the east,
in Eden; and there he put the man he had formed.
And the LORD God made all kinds of trees grow
out of the ground—trees that were pleasing to the eye
and good for food. In the middle of the garden
were the tree of life and the tree of the
knowledge of good and evil.
Genesis 2:7-9

CHICAGO OCCUPIES THIRTY-FIVE MILES of shoreline on Lake Michigan, one of the five so-called "Great Lakes." *Great* is the appropriate word, for these five remarkable lakes contain approximately 20 percent of the world's total surface fresh water supply. For years I've watched as rural agricultural pesticides, urban storm-drain overflow and exhaust-produced acid rain make their way into these great water basins. I've also observed the gradual clean-up of these lakes and the rebirth of the fishing and recreational industries as a result. Yet I hear many Christians crying for less environmental concern and fewer restrictions on the industrial and commercial activities that caused the problems in the first place. Does God care about these issues?

As a pastor and a father, I can hardly describe the pain I felt as I visited my people who lived in slum conditions. Baby cribs were pushed up against walls where old lead paint was cracking, curling and being broken off by the children, who would chew it like gum, sending toxins straight to their little brains and reducing their potential for life. Lead in paint is illegal now, of course. But old paints, like asbestos and lead pipes, still remain in many buildings and along with other code violations create enormous problems for urban families.

Is it enough to care only about the spiritual or eternal souls of kids under such circumstances? I didn't think so, but where in Scripture does one turn to start the discussion?

Many years ago I was invited to the Billy Graham Center at Wheaton College, along with a few other Chicago pastors, to discuss with college trustees how Wheaton might relate to the city and its troublesome issues. It was a very frank exchange. At one point a trustee said, "Ray, I get very excited when you, Bill (Leslie) and the others talk about evangelism in the city, but I get very nervous when you talk about social action, social justice and social involvement. Isn't that the social gospel?"

At first flush I felt some defensiveness, but then after a quick prayer for help I asked the businessman where he lived and why he lived there. He very calmly described his nice, safe, good, clean, suburban community where housing values increase and where he feels his family can be secure while he travels.

Finally, I said, "Every reason you've given for living where you live is a social reason. If those social systems of education, police and fire protection, economy and such didn't exist, you'd leave. If anybody believes in the social gospel, it's you! You've committed your whole life and family to those values."

His response was, "I never thought of that."

I went on to say that he and I agreed that all these social or public systems are important. The only difference was, his family had them while my family did not. Moreover, I suggested, if he were in my community, there would be no way he could say we evangelicals should just preach the gospel.

Frankly, there has been some hypocrisy in the evangelical community on these issues. I've watched Christians flock to the suburbs over the years so they could access the best our society could offer for their families, while raising suspicions about those of us who sought transformed communities of justice, peace, health and economic opportunity for those left behind. If we are brothers and sisters in Christ, how can we tolerate such disparities?

Much More Is Now at Stake

The issues are much larger today, because the majority of the world's Christians live outside the Western, developed rich countries. Christians struggling to see the whole world as God surely sees it have new reasons to ask how we can bridge the have-have not gaps between the nations of the world. These aren't just poor nations; they are poor nations with incredible numbers of new Christian brothers and sisters, who read the same Bible we do and expect it will make difference in both global and local relationships.

In this context we return to the opening photographs of the Bible and discover that God's hands are in the mud, making people out of earth's dirt (Gen 2:7). In his marvelous little book *Christianity and the Social Order,*[1] William Temple helped me see the theological significance of this photograph, as he calls it. It's so totally contrary to the pictures of other gods in the ancient world, which, like the Greek mythology, tended to put layers of protection between their spiritual deities and the physical matter of earth, lest the gods become contaminated.

Temple further observes that the Bible concludes with the photograph of our God cleaning up the cosmos after the final holocaust, and that this same Bible pictures a God who occupies real physical bodies, Christ's and ours. His conclusion: Christianity is the most materialistic religion on the entire earth. It's the only religion that successfully integrates matter and spirit with integrity.

After many years of teaching and preaching the Old Testament and learning from biblical theologians such as H. Wheeler Robinson and Walter Brueggemann, I am convinced that the ancient Hebrews had a holistic view of faith and world that today's Christians need to recover.[2] If Temple is correct, we Christians are the only people who can truly discuss the salvation of souls and the rebuilding of city sewer systems in the same sentence.

Sin has profoundly scarred the world as well as its people. A cursory reading in the history of civilizations does not present much optimism about the essential goodness of people and governments. Urban ministers need a reasonable hope. Progress is possible at times, but perfection will await Christ's return.

While in Genesis we read that God is connected to the earth, John 1:3 reminds us that Jesus Christ as God actually participated as the agent through which creation came into existence.

God Lives in Community and Works in Partnerships

In Ephesians 1 Paul describes "redemption activities" performed by each member of the Trinity that parallel the creation activities. The concept of Trinity suggests that God is three persons in an eternal set of relationships, three distinct yet interpenetrating persons in an eternal love bond, working on cooperative work projects. Paul reminds us that before the world was created, the Father chose us for salvation; then (two thousand years ago) the Son sacrificed his life for us; now the Spirit seals us like an engagement ring until the day of redemption.

Nothing can be clearer about the spiritual essence of the Trinity than that God lives in community and works in partnership for both the creation and the redemption of the world. Under the pressure of a billion "lost souls," however, many overly pragmatic Western

Christians have adopted a hierarchy of values—redemption over creation—for the sake of the evangelistic mandate. This hierarchy has created the great divorce and resulted in a canon within the canon of Scriptures—that is, while they believe the whole Bible is the Word of God, they treat certain parts as more valuable or useful than others. As a result, many Christians justify throwing away neighborhoods like styrofoam cups when they cease to function for our benefit. They deny that the salvation or destruction of communities is a spiritual issue.

Remember, you are never more like God than when you are living in relationships with God's people and working in partnerships for the re-creation and redemption of God's world.

A long-time colleague, Ed Dayton of World Vision, often reminded us that "a point of view is a view from a point." For evangelicals, the Great Commission of Jesus to go, evangelize and make disciples among the nations is a very significant command, and rightly so. We ought to obey our Lord. But which of the commission texts will we take as normative? Matthew 28:19, "Make disciples of all nations," focuses on the *ethnē* or peoples. Mark 16:15, on the other hand, says to "preach the good news to all creation."

Over the past twenty years I've been very active as a founder and chair of Evangelicals for Middle East Understanding, a group that includes many Orthodox believers. In Bible studies and conferences over those years, they have reminded me that God's redemption includes the whole *cosmos*, the whole creation.

In addition, as David Bosch points out in his magnificent missiological text *Transforming Mission*, the commission in Matthew 28:19 requires us to teach everything that Christ taught, and that includes both the social justice and the salvation texts.[3]

Clearly then, the Trinity doctrine helps to provide a practical spiritual foundation for urban ministry that includes some key ideas:

☐ God (Father, Son and Spirit) is not defiled by contact with the physical, even contaminated or toxic earth.

☐ God was planning and executing both the creation and the salvation work simultaneously.

☐ Creation and redemption are multigenerational, and we can be realistic about progress.

☐ It's not a sign of a superior spirituality to work alone personally or organizationally.

☐ There's no reason to assume God is present on a beautiful mountaintop but absent from the city. He's there in the stuff of local ministry.

Motives for Urban Ministry

There's more! Augustine notes that the fact that God is Trinity suggests entirely different motives for ministry than if he were just one being. Put simply, if God were one, then God needed to create Adam to experience love and a relationship for the first time. That is a high view of Adam but a very flawed view of God; a God who lacked love and *needed* to create Adam to meet his own needs. That God could be potentially manipulated by the creation to meet those needs. On the contrary, the Trinity always experienced loving relationships among themselves and created the world out of the overflow—the desire to share the grace with Adam and creation. That's a fundamentally different motive for God's creation.[4]

This discussion has guided my own sense of motives for urban ministry. I've concluded that I'm not in the city because the city is a place of great needs, even though it is that. I'm here because God has done a work of grace in my life that compels me to share. It overflows. Needs shape my priorities, of course, but are not the primary motives. If we are need-driven, we can become manipulated, even codependent on our ministries for identity, for security and, not the least of all, for funds. Sadly we've observed the burnout of many need-driven partners in the urban mission of the church over the years.

These creation texts don't stand alone, of course. Throughout this book we will return to the balance between the so-called social and spiritual aspects of ministry. In the meantime, we acknowledge that inner-city neighborhoods are often ugly, and the systems are broken. We all know a healthy person needs a healthy family, and a healthy family needs a healthy community. The tension will always be there between the need to spiritually transform persons and the need to socially transform places.

Yet there's a sense in which if Christ is with me in the midst of the slum, the neighborhood is a slum no longer. For Christ lives in me, and his kingdom agendas confront the neighborhood.

Celebrate it again: *"God's hands are in the mud!"* It's a very important idea for those called to be stewards of the earth and "Restorers of Streets with Dwellings" (Is 58:12).

3
CAN WE SAVE A CITY LIKE SODOM?

"What if only ten [righteous people]
can be found there?"
He answered, "For the sake of ten,
I will not destroy it."
Genesis 18:32

Now this was the sin of your sister Sodom:
She and her daughters were arrogant, overfed
and unconcerned; they did not help the poor and needy.
Ezekiel 16:49

CAN A HANDFUL OF PEOPLE save a city? Can a few leaven the multitudes?

For twenty years, since my first trip to Cairo, Egypt, in 1976, I've watched the Christian community grow in the seven garbage communities where nearly 100,000 very poor people live among the garbage they collect. These faithful Christians, multiplied now by thousands, have developed caring support systems in their community such as education and health care, as well as a strong infrastructure. Their witness impacts the whole city.

Simon Nandjui, a government official in Côte d'Ivoire, was framed and unjustly imprisoned. But he began preaching in that prison, and a revival broke out into a chain of house churches and ministries that are impacting Abidjan from prison to palace. I've seen the difference between 1986 and 1996.

Stephan de Beer, a young Afrikaner theological student, was led of God into a special concern for black street kids, worked with them and got them housed in a church, which some police officials allegedly torched. Eight of Stephan's kids died in the fire. But recently God used him to bring together a network of 150 urban leaders, black and white, for worship, teaching and reconciling in Pretoria, the very heart of Afrikanerdom.

Jember Teferra was the wife of the former mayor of Addis Ababa during the last years of Haile Selassie's reign in Ethiopia. The coup that overthrew the emperor landed Jember's husband in prison. She carried two meals a day to the prison for him for three years. Then she was put into a prison with 150 women who hated her privileged status. She spent five years in prison.

After her release, Jember went to England to earn a master's degree in community development. Then she went back to Ethiopia and has worked with up to 40,000 inner-city people, helping them build houses, working to provide schools, jobs, sewers, toilets and well-baby clinics. She has become the "conscience of the city" there in the slums, less famous than Teresa of Calcutta but like the women in Beirut and Belfast who are praising God and rebuilding their cities.

My stories could go on. Believe me when I say that ten Holy-Spirit-led men or women can pressure and even transform huge cities. It's happening everywhere. There is a relationship always between the *presence* of the godly and the *preservation* of urban communities.

The First Cities of the Bible

Sodom is mentioned more than fifty times in the Bible. People who know almost nothing about the Bible seem to know a great deal about this city, for its reputation for sex and violence has flourished in the worldwide film industry.

To the readers of Genesis, God's judgment on Sodom seems like a logical outcome. The first city was founded by Cain, who, after breaking fellowship with God, needed a human community to compensate for lost fellowship (Gen 4). Cain's violent genes required the rule of law but permitted the flourishing of the arts. From the outset cities appear to have been a mixed blessing.

Then, en route to our Sodom story, the city Babel (Gen 11) epitomizes the ill fate of urban greed and aggrandizement. Furthermore, if one needs the reinforcement of negative images, the Genesis writers report that Abraham, as he would later be called, was told to leave his own highly developed urban civilization at Ur on the Tigris-Euphrates delta and give himself to a life of migration, mostly to rural areas. The not-so-hidden meaning would seem to be: the good guys must leave the cities.

In this context, Abraham's prayer for Sodom is very significant, precisely because it's a prayer of negotiation with God to save a wicked city. And, in fact, God's response is that the city will indeed be saved *if* ten righteous residents can be found within it.

Throughout the Old Testament, Israel's theology carefully balances the individual and community, a fact noted in the fourth chapter of H. H. Rowley's marvelous study, *The Faith of Israel.*[1] The principle is clear: *The presence of godly people is beneficial for the salvation of places.* This is the Old Testament's witness to an idea mentioned by Jesus in Matthew 5, where the righteous are called to be both salt and light, which I've heard John Stott call "the twin vocations of the Christian."

In an era and climate of nonrefrigeration, salt was used as a preservative that worked its way down into the parts of the food most prone to rot and spoil. Light, on the other hand, must rise above to expose everything and ward off potential evil. Clearly, the witness of the righteous in ancient Israel included both these elements.

Strength Found in Community

Cities imply neighbors. When reading Deuteronomy again in this light, you'll notice it's a surprisingly urban book that emphasizes the importance of community. In chapter 22 you'll find some rather remarkable rape laws. If a woman was raped in a rural area, the people would execute the man who did it (vv. 25-27). If she was raped in the city, on the other hand, they would execute them both (vv. 23-24). Why? There was an assumption in Israel that city victims would cry for help, and neighbors would respond. If there was no response, the first assumption would have been that she didn't cry for help.

The law presumed that the presence of neighbors or community is beneficial to the security and salvation of individual persons. That's the role of the city system, with its walls, gates and code of law, but it's also the role of its righteous remnant.

When I became a pastor in Chicago, my first community service was the funeral of the neighboring pastor and wife two blocks down the street from my church. They had been stabbed to death during the night in what is still an unsolved crime. One of their three preschool children stopped the postman at the door the following morning and plaintively asked, "Can you wake up my daddy?" As I described the situation to my mother later that week, she asked—doubtless thinking of my own little boys—"How long are you going to stay in Chicago?"

I replied, "As long as I can count on other believers here. If I can't, I'll run far and fast."

I did not then nor do I now intend to trivialize this principle. I believe it and have been a committed member of a support group we call The Chicago Network that meets one morning a month and twice annually for overnight retreats. We have committed ourselves to each other for pastoral care and to our city for professional growth and public witness.

Why Was Sodom Destroyed?

Having recognized that the presence of righteous people can save a city, we must address the issue of why Sodom was destroyed. Most sermons I've heard over the years point to something like a gay-rights ordinance that permitted sexual behaviors that were totally out of control, immoral and perhaps illegal. I certainly do not want to commend Lot or condone the city for its sexual morals. But, according to the Bible, the city was not destroyed primarily for its sexual behaviors.

In the heart of Ezekiel 16 (an amazing chapter about cities that I'll discuss later in this book), Ezekiel gives us the divine commentary on the destruction of Sodom:

> As surely as I live, declares the Sovereign LORD, your sister Sodom and her daughters never did what you and your daughters have done.
>
> Now this was the sin of your sister Sodom: She and her daughters were arrogant, overfed and unconcerned; they did not help the poor and needy. They were haughty and did detestable things before me. Therefore I did away with them as you have seen. (Ezek 16:48-50)

The immediate context contrasts Sodom with the even greater debaucheries of Jerusalem, which faced its own punishing judgment at the hand of Babylon. What specifically was the terrible sin of Sodom that displeased Almighty God? The rich were getting richer and were proud of their extravagant surpluses while the poor were getting poorer. And because in the midst of their awful haughtiness they did not aid the poor and needy, God said, "I did away with them."

Let me ask a question: Do you know any city in the world where the rich are getting richer and the poor are getting poorer? In fact, if you are honest, you will confess, as I do, that we know of no city where the gap is *not* widening. That, my friend, is the most biblical sign that your city is in grave danger of God's judgment.

The Bible mentions the poor about 400 times, and studies have shown that there are many kinds of poverty and vulnerability. Raymond Fung, a Baptist Christian leader of Hong Kong, often says that the poor have a double problem: "The poor are not only sinners;

most often they are also the sinned against."

God is looking for a few righteous people who will live in every city. With this in mind, read Isaiah 59:14-21:

So justice is driven back,
    and righteousness stands at a distance;
truth has stumbled in the streets,
    honesty cannot enter.
Truth is nowhere to be found,
    and whoever shuns evil becomes a prey.
The LORD looked and was displeased
    that there was no justice.
He saw that there was no one,
    he was appalled that there was no one to intervene;
so his own arm worked salvation for him,
    and his own righteousness sustained him.
He put on righteousness as his breastplate,
    and the helmet of salvation on his head;
he put on the garments of vengeance
    and wrapped himself in zeal as in a cloak.
According to what they have done,
    so will he repay
wrath to his enemies
    and retribution to his foes;
    he will repay the islands their due.
From the west, men will fear the name of the LORD,
    and from the rising of the sun, they will revere his glory.
For he will come like a pent-up flood
    that the breath of the LORD drives along.
"The Redeemer will come to Zion,
    to those in Jacob who repent of their sins,"
declares the LORD.

    "As for me, this is my covenant with them," says the LORD.
"My Spirit, who is on you, and my words that I have put in your

mouth will not depart from your mouth, or from the mouths of your children, or from the mouths of their descendants from this time on and forever," says the LORD.

Why was God angry? More than angry—provoked, furious (v. 18). He saw the sins of Jerusalem, and no one would do anything about it. So God acted righteously, delivered the city, restored the communities for families and sent the Spirit to live in the city with them.

I don't need to tell American Christians that we live in a day of large-scale Christian withdrawal from large sections of our cities. The people running away from Los Angeles are bumping into the people running away from Chicago, somewhere in Colorado's pristine mountains, or so it seems at times. The results: the social gaps grow, God is furious, and our nation is at risk.

It should also be clear from the Sodom story that if God wishes you to be rescued from a city, the angels will find you. And if you continue to read about Sodom's destruction in Genesis 19, you'll observe that a relocation to the "suburbs" did not give Lot and his daughters a new morality. They carried the morality of the city with them. The daughters got their father drunk on two occasions, and he got them pregnant, which caused Edom and Moab to be born.

Now, remembering that ten people could have saved Sodom—and should have saved it, as both Abraham and God desired—consider God's words to Jerusalem before her exile: "Go up and down the streets of Jerusalem, look around and consider, search through her squares. If you can find but one person who deals honestly and seeks the truth, I will forgive this city" (Jer 5:1).

Just imagine the agony of God at the multiplied sins of Jerusalem. Now he's not asking for ten righteous; he's looking for just one righteous urbanite. That's all! The presence and righteous power of one person could have spared Jerusalem.

Praying for a City
Back in our Genesis account, Abraham faced Sodom and prayed

earnestly for it. We live in a time when God's people are discovering the power of prayer in and for cities. I remember well a July Sunday in 1985, walking through a slum in Surabaya, Indonesia. I was visiting a Christian family who lived there. Originally they had simply been assigned a weekly prayer walk in this slum of Muslim refugees from the island of Madura. Prayer walks are generally times when believers covenant to walk about a certain section of the city and pray for everything, including houses, people and families, with eyes open, pleading for God to shed grace and salvation on that community. This dear couple got so burdened during their walking-about prayers that they moved into the community and had a phenomenal ministry there—a ministry that I still find hard to describe and impossible to explain.

And also, in our time, God's people are organizing to confront the strongholds of the city, be they commercial, political, educational or even cultural. Exorcism is a valid ministry, and because Christ has confronted and defeated the principalities and powers, has unmasked them and has rescued us from Satan's evil empire, we need not fear, but we will respect those concentrations of demonic power that remain in our cities. Of course, the Christians of the earliest centuries reminded us that spiritual warfare can and should also be done in deserts.

Many contemporary discussions of prayer overlook this link with the righteous remnant who are called to live within these communities as salt and light.[2] While prayer is right and critical for a city's survival, it can never be a substitute for the conscious relocation of Christians to set up residency and witness in the midst of the evil. Nehemiah went to the suburbs and small towns intentionally to recruit a tithe (one out of ten) of good, capable resource people for relocation into the city (Neh 11:1-2). He prayed for it and worked on it, but then he asked healthy communities to tithe their human resources into neighborhoods of need.

Personally, I don't believe pastors have preached tithing biblically until they have a strategic plan to call members into the church's local community. Yes, that too is being done now. We're seeing it coast to coast in the USA. Educated suburbanites and rural Christians are choosing to follow God and are making downward social mobility an art form for the sake of a righteous witness in corrupt urban communities. A tithe of nonurbanites is enough, however. More than that can intimidate the local community and begin to gentrify the community rather than transform it.

Can we save cities like Sodom? Of course we can, and we must. Thankfully the preserving effect of a few righteous people is much more widespread than we might think.

4
A SURPRISING SOURCE OF URBAN LEADERS
MOSES & HIS MOTHER

Now a man of the house of Levi married a Levite woman,
and she became pregnant and gave birth to a son.
When she saw that he was a fine child, she hid him
for three months. But when she could hide him no longer,
she got a papyrus basket for him and coated it
with tar and pitch. Then she placed the child in it
and put it among the reeds along the bank of the Nile.
Exodus 2:1-3

I'VE WITNESSED A VERITABLE DELUGE of books on leadership in the decades of my ministry. Some, like Greenleaf's *Servant Leadership*, have broadened the metaphors or images of leadership. James McGregor Burns has helped clarify the differences between transforming and transactional leadership, reminding us that healthy organizations need both. Leadership research abounds, and each year we learn some new insights and buzzwords![1]

On the other hand, the Bible has always had much to say about leadership. In my first year of ministry I read *Why Jesus Never Wrote A Book*, by W. E. Sangster, a famous Methodist preacher from London. The book title came from his essay based on Mark 3:14 (KJV): "And he chose twelve that he might be with them." For Jesus, leadership was something to be caught as well as taught.[2] There is a contagion to leadership development.

One might think that to inaugurate a significant worldwide ministry you would need to focus attention on the crowds, solving crisis after crisis. In contrast, the Gospels show Jesus spending 50 percent of his three-year ministry time with twelve people and perhaps another 25 percent with only three people—Peter, James and John. So, I surmised, to lead God's church in megacities, I should think small. That was quite contrary to the leadership literature I was reading.

It was almost another conversion experience for me when I studied and began to reflect seriously on Moses and his mom during the class I was taking on the Pentateuch at Trinity Evangelical Divinity School. I observed that God's liberation of Israel and the great exodus movement began with poor urban women who broke the law by having illegal babies. The law, genocidal and totally unjust, made this a case of civil disobedience.

Moses' mother had a baby and couldn't raise him. Her husband was unable to solve the problem. So she made a little boat, floated her kid down the Nile, got him rescued and was paid to raise him. She beat the system!

Later I was to pastor many public aid or welfare mothers. Oh, how I admired them, watching them raise their kids on limited funds and food stamps in tough situations, often taking abuse, yet surviving and bringing their children as an offering to the Lord at my church. Moses' mom became my patron saint for welfare moms.

The Education of an Urban Leader

Moses meanwhile grew up biculturally, and, according to Stephen (Acts 7:22), he "was educated in all the wisdom of the Egyptians." He must have had a formidable geometry, history and philosophy background!

Although some may disagree at this point, let me remind you of something Moses, Daniel, Esther, Nehemiah and a host of biblical luminaries appear to have had in common. None of them was home schooled. In fact, on the contrary, they seem to have been educated in so-called pagan educational systems to the glory of God for public leadership in their respective cultures.

Please understand that my lament is for the nearly wholesale withdrawal by Christians from presence in and positive local engagement with public or common urban school systems. Clearly, there are situations where private schools or personal tutoring are needed.

Much is wrong with urban school systems, of course. I routinely argue, myself, that they are designed not as educational systems but as revenue recruitment or employment systems. Those systems are nearly impervious to reform on the basis of educational criteria, such as "What really is best for these children?"

Like Moses, Joseph, Daniel, Nehemiah and others were able to sort through the public, ethical differences between cobelligerency and advocacy on issues and survived as capable leaders working for corrupt politicians. As an aside, I should point out that one of the five Antioch international pastoral team members (Acts 11:19—13:1) was Manean, a political associate of Herod. Imagine Paul serving on a church staff where a pastoral colleague was on the payroll of one of the Herods.

But we who live and work in cities are not surprised by this. We know that every city-centered church needs political skills. In fact, urban schools like Moody Bible Institute could not have functioned in a highly structured political matrix like Chicago for a century without highly skilled legal, political and financial savvy. Those are the lessons nearly every graduate of these schools (like me) needs but is seldom taught. Land banking (saving and even acquiring new church property in urban real estate markets that often prove prohibitive to new church growth), negotiating, crisis and conflict management, and fundraising are all part of the urban leader's tool kit. Christian schools generally shroud such "institutional behaving" activities in secret while teaching "institutional believing" activities. It's safer to decontextualize theological education, I guess. Why else would we perpetuate it when it so obviously limits students' access to the real issues in urban ministry?

Through his training Moses learned how to run Egypt and its institutions, even though he was an Israelite by birth. Then he went through a crisis of identity, even committing an act of violence. A lot of leaders or potential leaders play the game, get the degree by leaving their own community and its culture, only to snap under the pressure of this dichotomy. Moses snapped, lashed out and fled. Some of the 1960s "rage literature," such as *Soul on Ice* or *Manchild in the Promised Land,* could have been written about Moses.[3]

Leadership Through Crosscultural Learning

Then followed a critical postgraduate experience for Moses in the desert, where he learned sheep culture, desert language and literature, and public health in primitive communities. I myself once took a college microbiology course entitled "Public Health in Primitive Communities." My wife can attest to its usefulness during the last thirty-plus years of inner-city living and ministry!

Finally, after having spent two-thirds of his life in preparation that was academic, contextual and experientially integrated, Moses was ready for leadership. God could now use him to lead a group of mud-brick makers and their community into the worst neighborhoods of the Middle East where he would build a culture and a faith for the people.

Moses' huge community was largely unemployed and survived on "food-stamp" manna provisions for forty years. Moses had to be a realist about resources. He did human development that led to community and economic development and prepared a migrant group to occupy a foreign land. I still chuckle at the reported comment made by former Israeli Prime Minister Golda Meir: "Moses was not a good leader. He led our people all over the Middle East and settled on the only real estate without oil."

As a classically trained professional, which probably accentuated his sense of call and superior expertise, he organized the people to be completely dependent on him (Ex 18). The greatness of Moses as a leader is revealed in the fact that he was able to be taught and could listen to God and the people. From his father-in-law, Jethro, he learned how to organize and multiply leadership by giving it away. He learned a simple truth I read in Gamson's *Power and Discontent* back in the seventies: power is merely the ability to get things done, and it is expandable.[4]

When I first read the entire narrative of Israel's journey from Egypt to the Promised Land in Exodus through Deuteronomy, focusing on how Moses learned, behaved and modeled leadership, I was overwhelmed. In Exodus 31 and 35 we find the first gift of the Holy Spirit mentioned in the entire Bible—an art committee composed of Bezaliel and Oholiab, former mud-straw brick makers who were gifted for crafts, beauty and design. Why? Why does a poor, unemployed migrant group on public aid for food need the arts? Luther knew the reason when he expressed that the poor need beauty as much as they need bread, because they live in ugliness. Moses let the arts emerge, and along with them health laws to address environmental concerns.

Read Leviticus and see how pluralistic the forms of worship were in sensitivity for the poor. One worship size did not fit all, even in the pressure-cooker environment of a migrant group amid hostile neighbors.

The View from the Mountaintop

Moses learned from his mistakes, and he lived with the consequences (just read the book of Numbers). Finally we see him in his last photograph, standing on the mountain overlooking Jericho and the Jordan and looking west toward the Promised Land (Deut 34). On this mountaintop we gaze back toward Egypt with Moses to see his geographical and historical perspective.

In chapter three of *The Unheavenly City Revisited,* an exploration of the relationship of time to social class, Edward Banfield reminds us that people who cannot remember cannot set goals.[5] The creative way forward is a creative way backward in memory. Henri Nouwen agrees in his beautiful little devotional book *The Living Reminder.*[6] He notes that the prophets tell us to prepare for the future, but they do so by telling us (over ninety times) to remember the past.

Urban leaders need to see the big picture. Somewhere Augustine wrote that for the Christian "the past is a present memory, and the future is a present possibility." Moses was a three-dimensional person that I've come to admire tremendously. You can never know enough to be a leader of the urban poor, but my testimony is that you can never pay for the education they will give you if you let them.

Moses would agree, I'm sure. He reminds us that you don't have to grow up in this wilderness to lead the people there, but you'd better include some of the indigenous folks on the leadership team. Likewise, urban leaders need not and often do not originate in cities. Karl Barth reminds us that grace is an outside gift. Urban leaders are often, though not always, grace gifts from other environments. Moses was among the first, but not nearly the last, in redemptive history to demonstrate that God still calls people to crosscultural leadership with all the strengths and limitations implicit in this model.

The picture of Moses on Mount Nebo in Deuteronomy 34 is that of this larger-than-life leader doing theological reflection in solitude. Looking south, back toward Egypt, he can reflect on life's surprising journey and the grace of God in his life. Looking west across the Jordan valley, he can see the future where he is not privileged to go (for he will die on the edge of the Promised Land).

The purpose for "mountaintop" experiences is not escape but perspective. Moses has trained his successors. They are standing by. New gifts will be needed, as they are for each generation of ministry in cities and everywhere.

Although I've spent thirty-eight years of ministry exclusively in urban centers, after growing up in a very rural place amid immigrant and ethnic Americans, I'm still an outsider to the city I love. Moses has mirrored many of my anxieties and shared many of his coping strategies with me. The grace continues.

5
HOPE IN THE CITY
THE STORY OF RUTH

In the days when the judges ruled,
there was a famine in the land. . . .
The women said to Naomi:
"Praise be to the LORD, who this day
has not left you without a kinsman-redeemer."
Ruth 1:1; 4:14

LET'S FACE IT. OUR CITIES ARE spiraling downward. In many of its communities, Chicago looks far worse than when I arrived more than thirty years ago. Crack cocaine, AIDS and assault weapons are taking an increasing toll on our cities. The profile of street people has cycled again, leaving mothers with children as the fastest growing group of the homeless.

Everyone in America now knows that children are killing children. Last year in Chicago an eleven-year-old boy nicknamed "Yummy" killed a fourteen-year-old. Then Yummy was himself executed—and buried with his teddy bear.

Governments are downsizing and privatizing services, yet the budgets of the not-for-profit ministries and service organizations can't possibly pick up all the slack. Many who used to help are not there. When an apathy called "compassion fatigue" describes the outsiders and "burnout" describes the insiders, a kind of numbing hopelessness settles into the consciousness of urban churches.

If you want to be seriously depressed, read Jonathan Kozol's *Amazing Grace: The Lives of Children and the Conscience of a Nation,* the extraordinary story of the death culture emerging among kids in South Bronx, New York.[1] Then read the Old Testament book of Judges, with special attention to the last four chapters.

Judges provides the candid background to Israel's sad history between the time of Joshua and the monarchy of King Saul. The "dark ages" described in Judges can be characterized as seven eras in each of which God delivered Israel, with the help of a leader called a judge, and then the people reverted to sinful ways and fell into oppression, only to need deliverance again. The author of Judges closes his account by summarizing these seven eras—spanning nearly 400 years—with the phrase "In those days Israel had no king; everyone did as he saw fit" (21:25).

History for Israel was going nowhere but moving in vicious cycles, climaxing in the gruesome story of the Bethlehem concubine who was "gang-banged" all night and left for dead in the streets of Gibeah. Her master then cut her into twelve parts and "mailed" one part of her butchered body to each of the twelve tribes of Israel. Talk about a wake-up call!

That's the sobering context for the story of Ruth. All the domestic abuse and violence, the economic and political failure sound familiar to today's urban dwellers. Ruth gives us the clues for reading this awful history and making sense of it. Ruth is a story of hope for the meantime, which is a "mean time," between the great acts of God in the past and the great acts of God in the future.[2]

Ruth is one of two books in the Bible named for a woman. The other is Esther. Surprisingly, perhaps, both tell the story of an interracial second marriage. Ruth, a Moabite and a descendant of Sodom, is choreographed into the early history of Israel by becoming the great-grandmother of Israel's greatest king and an ancestor of Jesus on his earthly side (Mt 1:5). Esther, a diaspora Jew, marries into the Persian monarchy, and her story becomes a commentary on the latter history of Israel.

The book of Ruth may best be described as a biblical soap opera with each chapter as an act in the drama. Let me sketch the story briefly.

Prologue. With quick brush strokes, the author sets the scene by telling us there was a famine in Bethlehem (which means "house of bread") during the time of the judges. Elimelech ("God is my king") took Naomi ("pleasant") and their two sick kids, Mahlon and Kilion ("sickly" and "dying"), to Moab for salvation from the famine. There in Moab, off the map of Bethlehem and Judah, "God is my king" died along with his two sons. The situation fits with the whole tone of Judges. God seems to be out of the picture, and so in this upside-down era, the godly go to Moab (Sodom's ancestral land) seeking hope.

Act One, Scene One. As our drama opens, three women—Naomi (no longer pleasant), Ruth and Orpah, her Moabite daughters-in-law—are weeping. (I told you it is a soap opera!) Naomi has decided to return to Bethlehem but wants her foreign daughters-in-law to stay in Moab. Perhaps she knew how difficult it would ultimately be to bury them in a Jewish cemetery back home. Orpah listens and stays; Ruth does not. Her magnificent plea (1:16-17) has become a familiar wedding song in our own day. And so, as Scene One closes, two women head north from Moab into modern Jordan, down through Jericho and up the road to Jerusalem, then south to Bethlehem—a journey no women should have taken alone, because "it was the time of the judges."

Act One, Scene Two. Bethlehem, days later. Two women straggle into town. Seeing them from afar, the village women gather in the streets and ask, "Can this be Naomi?"

" 'Don't call me Naomi,' she told them. 'Call me Mara ["bitter"], because the Almighty has made my life very bitter' " (1:20).

This first act portrays a vicious cycle. It starts and ends in Bethlehem, first without bread and now without the men of the family. Ancient historians generally thought history moved in cycles. Their writing used the analogies of the life cycle—birth, growth, maturity, decline and death—or the seasons—spring, summer, fall and winter. Only Hereclitus the Greek is reported to have disagreed. Contrary to his contemporaries, his view, "You can't step into the same river twice," argued that history moves toward a goal.

Ruth 1, like the Book of Judges, raises the question: Is that all there is? Is life just a vicious cycle? Not surprisingly, the experience of most city people leads them to ask these same questions.

Act Two, Scene One. Harvest time in Bethlehem. Naomi instructs Ruth on Israel's welfare system. The poor and other undocumented aliens are permitted to glean around the edges of any field.

Act Two, Scene Two. Ruth just "happens" to enter the field of Bethlehem's most eligible bachelor, Boaz, who also just "happens" to be there that day. If Act One raises the question of whether history runs in cycles, Act Two presents the question of whether history is an accident, the result of chance. Boaz gets emotionally involved quickly, but Ruth gleans "ephods" of wheat naively unaware and returns to Naomi with her proceeds.

Act Three, Scene One. A mother-in-law and daughter-in-law discuss the "facts of life." Naomi issues three initial instructions: (1) take a bath; (2) use perfume; (3) wear your best dress. She then sends Ruth out to trap Boaz, who will be sleeping by his grain pile to protect it from being stolen during the night. (Remember, it was the time of the judges.) Boaz will eat, drink and then sleep. Ruth will sneak up, uncover him, and then sit upwind so that the perfume will waft its way into his nostrils. He'll wake up at midnight, see her looking like an angel in the moonlight and propose marriage.

This third act raises the question whether history is a conspiracy. It seems to advocate a "do-unto-others-before-they-do-unto-you" kind of philosophy.

What happens next? Don't ask; the curtain falls.

Act Four, Scene One. The city gates (which I can legitimately translate as "city hall"). It's the public, civic square inside the gated and walled city, where caravans discharge their wares and where all business and government officials can be found (see Prov 31:1-31). I think this is an appropriate interpretation of Matthew 16:18—"I will build my church, and the gates [city hall] of Hades will not overcome it."

Marriage laws in ancient Israel were bound up with family land ownership, so Boaz was technically announcing Naomi's land sale; the purchase price included Ruth. Moreover, the land would pass on to Naomi and Ruth's descendants. Eligible buyers included the closest relatives. Naomi had one closer relative. After calculating the cost, perhaps, this man walked away, leaving Boaz to redeem the land and marry Ruth.

Act Four, Scene Two. A baby shower. The village women we saw in chapter 1 are now passing around baby Obed, and Naomi is "pleasant" again. The book ends with ten names. Those names provide the interpretive clue to the terrible history of the time of the judges. Notice the last four names: Boaz, Obed, Jesse, David. Period. Full stop. End of book. This baby is the promise that a king is coming—the deliverer, the greatest king Israel will ever have is the great-grandson of this Moabite widow and will be the salvation of her mother-in-law. History is not circular; it's not an accident; it's not even a conspiracy. It is moving toward a goal: the salvation of God's people.

Changing Perspective and Gaining Meaning

I love the way the Orthodox church leaders summarize the salvation story in Scripture. For them the gospel in both testaments begins with "baby announcements." In Genesis 18, Sarah will have a baby. In Matthew 1, Mary will have a baby. She will be the "mother of God."

City churches rise, and they also decline over time. That's our reality. It's common today to measure church growth horizontally by size, budgets and numbers. Pastors and denominations under pressure to grow often encourage churches to abandon communities experiencing the "Judges phenomenon." In the name of the Great Commission, we are often challenged to this kind of "horizontal growth."

There is another perspective on the Great Commission that the Orthodox church embraces. It is the vertical growth of faithful believers over many generations.

America is essentially an optimistic culture. We expect to succeed, sometimes even despite obstacles. Now, however, we are hearing voices saying that Generation X and younger generations of Americans will not achieve the financial successes of their parents (usually white Americans are meant, I think). More and more wealthy Americans are retreating into "gated communities" to hold on to the tokens of privilege our society has bestowed on them.

Over time urban Christians have learned some lessons under pressure. Urban churches may be not so much victims as research-and-development units for recovering a spirituality for the future, a tempered realism to check the nervously held optimism of other Christians in our time. History is moving toward a goal. Ruth provides a hopeful lens on urban places that look like Judges. God still moves in mysterious ways his wonders to perform. In the divine choreography of history, I am reminded of the line in the Christmas hymn: "How silently, how silently the wondrous gift is given, when God imparts to human hearts the blessings of his heaven."

6
THE INDIVIDUAL &
THE COMMUNITY
DO WE FIND A THEOLOGY
OF PLACE IN THE BIBLE?

Go up and down the streets of Jerusalem,
look around and consider,
search through her squares.
If you can find but one person
who deals honestly and seeks the truth,
I will forgive this city.
Jeremiah 5:1

AT THIS POINT I'D LIKE to take a step back from examining Old Testament texts individually to take a broader look at the Hebrew worldview that connected people to the context of their places and families.

The evangelicalism I grew up with had a theology of persons and programs, but it lacked a conscious theology of place. Protestants generally had cut themselves off from "parish" thinking—an ongoing commitment to their *place* of ministry—so that when a church's location became "inconvenient" it simply relocated to a new place, often near a freeway (reflecting our society's shift from a walking to an automobile culture). Along the way, we abandoned real estate that had been prayed for fervently by Christians before us—and along with it abandoned any commitment to the neighborhoods we left behind.

I think it is much more than a practical, operational church decision when a church relocates in such a manner. It is a theological bias toward Greek individualism and away from a biblical holistic theology, which for me includes not only the physical aspects of persons but also the geography in which we have identity and security.

Does God care only about people, or does he also care about places, including cities? And if the Holy Spirit of Christ is in us, should we also care for both urban people and urban places?

Historians and scholars have long recognized and even exploited the differences between the Greek emphasis on the individual and the Hebrew concept of community. Early in the twentieth century, H. Wheeler Robinson coined the expression "corporate solidarity" to describe what he saw as "the synthetic grasping of a totality" in the thought of ancient Israel.[1]

Theologian Otto Baab explains, regarding man, that

his whole being is inextricably bound up with the life of the entire community. Hence man appears as a corporate personality rather than as an individual. Such social entities as family, clan, tribe and nation must be examined if man is to be understood.[2]

Of course, like any theme, the importance of community in Scripture can be overstated.[3] H. H. Rowley presents a balanced picture, showing that while Jeremiah and Ezekiel stressed individual responsibility, they did not discover it—in all periods of Israel's history both the individual and the collective are stressed.[4]

Corporate solidarity is quite apparent throughout the Old Testament. First, the ancient Israelites identified a family with its ancestors. William Henry Green's studies in biblical genealogies showed that individual names often stood for family trees.[5] S. A. Cook has observed this as well.[6]

There is a bond between the generations, both past and future, and one cannot explain the Decalogue (Ex 20:5; Deut 5:9-10) without seeing that in Israel people inherited both the debits and the credits of previous generations.[7] Furthermore, in the Old Testament the names of people take on a special significance. In Israel, the son bore the dignity or the shame of the father, so that there is a theology of the name.[8]

The family unit was also highly valued in ancient Israel. The man of the house was the *baal,* owner, lord and completely responsible for that household. Abraham heard that the land would be for him and his offspring (Gen 12:7).

The relationship of the family to the larger national context must be interpreted with respect to this solidarity as well. Thus, tribes come from families and combine to form a nation.[9] So there is a cumulative effect here as the sin of Achan implicates the family but also costs the whole nation ultimately.[10]

The City as Old Testament Symbol of Corporate Solidarity

Several clues to the doctrine of "corporate personality" emerge in the context of urban life depicted in Scripture. First, the Old Testament city is implicated in its entirety whenever idolatry exists, even in incipient form, within its walls. The penalty appears harsh; the entire city is to be burned as an offering to the Lord (Deut 13:15–16). The principle is clear: the whole is contaminated by the part, and all must suffer the consequences. Naturally, this procedure worked both ways, making it incumbent upon all to guard against false doctrine which, in turn, would reinforce the authority of the commandments.

In addition, the city was wholly accountable for its moral standards, that is, for the individual conduct of those citizens who resided within its walls. This meant that the loss of virginity of a single girl could, under some circumstances, become a public issue (Deut 22:15). Disobedient children were somehow accountable to a public trust and disciplined or purged accordingly (Deut 21:20-21). With respect to morals, moreover, the presence of people was presumed to be good (and this will surprise the modern reader), a genuine guard against crime, such as a deterrent for rape (Deut 22:23-24).

As we discussed earlier, the ministry of ten good people can save a city or the lack of good people damn it (Gen 18). This is the clear teaching of Scripture in the evaluation of David's ministry, when Jerusalem was preserved for David's sake (2 Kings 19:34). Remembering Rowley's admonition, however, we should observe that the presence of a Job or Daniel in a city may not necessarily preserve it forever (Ezek 14:12-20), and even the godly Josiah and the revival in Jerusalem could not undo the consequences of generations of increased iniquity (2 Kings 23:26). Yet 120,000 children and cattle were a de facto preservative in the metropolitan situation of Nineveh, a fact that had to be explained to the prophet Jonah (Jon 4:11).

Furthermore, the mother-daughter relationship that biblical cities had with their related villages implies corporate solidarity (2 Sam 20:19; Is 1:8; Mic 1:13; Ezek 16:45-58; Lam 2:13).

A city, namely Jerusalem itself, became a symbol of God's presence and power in the world. G. A. F. Knight argues that Israel is a unity rather than a unit—"an extending organism."[11] If a city is anything, at least in idealized form, it is an organic, dynamic series of relationships, interwoven in a common crucible. This is the form in which the New Testament writers speak of Jerusalem, the "city of peace" (holy city). "The Jerusalem that is above is free" (Gal 4:26), and Christians are citizens of a heavenly city (Phil 3:20). There is indeed, at Mount Zion, a city of the Living God, a heavenly Jerusalem (Heb 12:22; 13:14); a new Jerusalem which comes down (Rev 21—22), in which God will be present in a unique sense, a sense vaguely realized in the Old Testament city of Jerusalem.

It was clearly taught in the Old Testament that Jerusalem was something special, for it was the place that God had ordained and where his name would dwell (Deut 12:11), and even in ruins (Is 44:5; 49:16) affirmations could be made on its behalf and its future could be anticipated (Zech 8:21; Ps 86:9).

City Solidarity: Some Ministry Applications

If the Bible teaches that cities are important beyond the fact that they are collections of individuals, then our ministry in cities must be both public and private, personal and corporate.

The Old Testament is not silent on the role of the religious leaders of God's people in the urban context. The following catalog of duties performed by Israel's religious leaders in cities is derived almost entirely from the historical books. It is not complete, nor has every context been studied critically with this in view. However, even a superficial study reveals that the concept of ministry in Israel, stemming from cities that symbolize a measure of corporate solidarity, was far more varied than we might otherwise have supposed.

How is it that the New Testament disciples became urban apostles? One way was by reading examples of ministry in urban contexts in the Old Testament itself. Israel's leaders did more than just "preach the gospel." They served the community in these ways:

Ministering to the sick. Elijah (1 Kings 17) and Elisha (2 Kings 4:18-37; 8:1-6) are both involved here.

Pastoral care. In the marital problem (Ezra 9) and in the midst of psychological warfare (2 Chron 32:18).

Counseling kings and national leaders. Hilkiah's (2 Chron 34:8-33) and Isaiah's roles in Hezekiah's reign (2 Kings 19).

Confronting kings with judgment. Micaiah had such a role (2 Chron 18; 1 Kings 22) as did Nathan (2 Sam 12).

Negotiating with armies. Elisha (2 Kings 6).

Keeping and collecting records (1 Chron 9). Actually, this is the point of the genealogies which recorded the continuing inheritance, blessing or cursing of families.

Interpreting local, national and world events. Hanani the seer (2 Chron 16:7); Isaiah (2 Kings 20), along with all the prophets.

Public proclamation of God's Word. Jehoshaphat (2 Chron 20:14-21).

Maintaining public worship. Solomon (1 Chron 7); Josiah (2 Chron 35:16-19). The importance of this service lies in the great detail given to the temple, dedication, repair and corporate worship.

Directing religious education. A mobile teaching program (2 Chron 17:7-9); a resident program (2 Chron 19:10). Both texts show the results were wholly beneficial.

Organization and administration of institutions and festivals. The priests were divided into administrative units (2 Chron 23:4-10; Neh 11:10-24).

Supervising the tithe storehouses (Neh 12:44). The Levites supervised the contiguous farmlands that belonged to cities and were so assigned by Moses (Num 35:2-5).

Distributing public welfare (2 Chron 31:15). According to the Pentateuch, the Levites were assigned forty-eight cities. Six of these were cities of refuge to which the refugees could flee for food, shelter and other provisions.

Training young prophets (1 Sam 10:5). Note also the ministry of Elijah, his influence on his successor and the prophets' school.

Providing for the entire ministerial staff. Priests were given responsibility for securing enough provisions to feed the choir members and maintenance men (Neh 10:39).

Confronting a street gang (2 Kings 2:23). In this text, the word *naharim* indicates that these were not children but a roving band of more than forty-two teens or young men who came "out of the city" (typical of groups that cavort in Chicago?).

Serving jury duty (2 Chron 19:5-8). Citywide implementation of the law required this at the instigation of the king.

Supervision of building projects. Temple repair (2 Chron 34:8-13) and altar rebuilding (Ezra 3:1-3). Nehemiah served a stint as architect, contractor (Neh 2:8) and inspector (Neh 2:13).

Delivering eulogies at state funerals. Note Jeremiah's part in Josiah's public funeral in 609 B.C. (2 Chron 35:25).

Delivering apologetic messages to unbelievers. Ezra can be seen in a public defense of God's work before a pagan audience (Ezra 8—9).

Holding dedication services (Ezra 7:15-17; Neh 12:27-43). Of course, the role of religious leaders was significant before the fall of Jerusalem also, but the kings were in the limelight.

Private and public prayer (Ezra 9:3—10:1). See also other passages in the historical books where prophets' prayers are recorded.

Publishing messages for wider audiences (Neh 8:15). Inter-city carriers were a necessary part of the Old Testament epoch.

Promoting urban renewal projects. In "renewal" one can see not only the building, reconstruction, and relocation of population groups, but renewal of the life as well. Both senses occur in the prophets. (See Nehemiah's role in moving the people back into Jerusalem amid the rubble, to make Jerusalem a "model city" [Neh 11:1] and the subsequent preaching for renewal of the heart in the later prophets.)

The religious duties in Israel included far more than preaching, while at the same time affirming the important role of the city in the amplification of the prophet's message. Urban sins made for national examples and national consequences in the Old Testament. The religious leaders stayed in the cities for the most part, affecting entire populations by life and even by death (1 Kings 13:31-32).

The Whole Church, the Whole Gospel, the Whole City

This emphasis on the importance of place, however, should not be misunderstood as parochialism. It is not enough to preach to and pray for our own city and not care about other cities. By contrast, the Lausanne Covenant initiated by Billy Graham and written chiefly by John R. W. Stott in 1974 put its articles on "Christian Social Responsibility" and "The Church and Evangelism" together, as indeed they must be.[12] Of course, I will admit that not everyone is called to do everything in every city.

God's kingdom agenda seeks the personal salvation of all persons *and* the social transformation of all places. Churches are both signs of and a witness to God's creative and redemptive agendas. We need the urban evangelist, the pastor and urban community developer as partners. None should assume their calling more spiritual or more significant than the other. Every gift belongs in the urban mission of the church.

7
ZION SONGS &
URBAN POETS
THE NEED FOR
TIMELESS TRUTH

Great is the LORD, and most worthy of praise,
in the city of our God, his holy mountain.
It is beautiful in its loftiness,
the joy of the whole earth.
Like the utmost heights of Zaphon is Mount Zion,
the city of the Great King.
God is in her citadels;
he has shown himself to be her fortress.
Psalm 48:1-3

NEARLY FORTY YEARS AGO I had the privilege of studying theology
for three years under J. C. Macaulay at Moody Bible Institute. One
of the many lessons I learned from him was the need for pastors to
be pastored themselves. He suggested we consider adopting a
venerable time-tested preacher as our pastor and read one of his
sermons every day to help sustain us in our ministry. His own
mentor was Alexander Maclaren, so I went out and bought the ten
large volumes of Maclaren's *Expositions of Holy Scripture,*[1] which had
just been republished by Eerdmans in 1959, and his three-volume work
on the Psalms, which I found in a used book store. (My vice was and
still is buying books.)

Maclaren's exposition of Psalm 23 hit me between the eyes one
day shortly thereafter. He suggested the psalm was autobiographical of both aspects of David's life. Scene one depicts David, the rural

shepherd, through verse four. Scene two is set at a state dinner in the palace banquet hall, where David is king, anointed and dwelling in God's house forever.

Eventually I found Claus Westerman and others teaching that many of the Psalms were composed for public celebrative worship in the heart of the city.[2] As I read further, I noticed in the imagery of other psalms that God chose to live in the city of Jerusalem and could be found occupying and even animating its institutions (see Ps 48).

Wisdom for Urban Living

Another light went on for me some twenty-five years ago when I was preparing a series of sermons and Sunday-school lessons on Proverbs, Ecclesiastes and Song of Solomon for my inner-city congregation. Rabbi Robert Gordis, a specialist on Hebrew poetry, had written a magnificent study of the Hebrew text of Ecclesiastes called *Koheleth: The Man and His World*.[3] I will paraphrase and slightly embellish a story he told to show the distinctive perspective of the Hebrew wisdom literature: Job, Psalms, Proverbs, Ecclesiastes and Song of Solomon.

Gordis begins, "While traveling down a street in Old Jerusalem, I meet an old priest. I ask him, 'Old priest, when are the good days?' The old priest responds, eyes glazed over with nostalgia, 'In the days of Moses, when the memory of Exodus was fresh and God was feeding us every day. Those were the good days.'" Gordis comments, "In the Divine Library (Holy Scripture) there is a body of literature that looks backward to the great acts of God in the past. This is the memory tradition of the Bible, a spirituality for those who 'back into the future.'"

As Gordis continues down the streets of old Jerusalem, he meets an old prophet and asks, "Old Prophet, when are the good days?" The old prophet's eyes glaze over with nostalgia, and he retorts, "In the future, when the Messiah will reign and all injustice and suffering will cease." Gordis adds, "In the Divine Library we also have a body of literature that looks forward to the great acts of God in the future."

As our narrator continues down the streets of Old Jerusalem, he meets an old sage, the Hebrew wise man and poet. He asks again, "When are the good days?" The old poet's eyes glaze over with nostalgia, he throws his hands up in the air and cries out, "Enjoy! Enjoy! It will never get any better; it will never get any worse." Says Gordis, the poetry of the Bible is a timeless wisdom literature for the present. It's existential, written for me, my feelings and my needs. Hebrew poetry is for the meantime—those "meantimes" such as the time of Judges, when God's people find themselves between the great acts of God in the past and the great acts of God in the future.

Then came the bombshell for me, when Gordis said that the golden age of Hebrew poetry was after the captivity, when the returned exiles had to live in the ruins of the old city surrounded by memories of God at work in the past, but knowing also that no miracles would occur for a long time to come.[4]

Now I knew why my people needed timeless, noncontextual theological truths in my inner-city neighborhood church. Our ravaged community looked worse every year. It was out of control and depressing. Pithy proverbs week after week gave welcome relief and surprising hope to my people.

Let's try something. Read Psalm 38 through.

O LORD, do not rebuke me in your anger
    or discipline me in your wrath.
For your arrows have pierced me,
    and your hand has come down upon me.
Because of your wrath there is no health in my body;
    my bones have no soundness because of my sin.
My guilt has overwhelmed me
    like a burden too heavy to bear.

My wounds fester and are loathsome
    because of my sinful folly.
I am bowed down and brought very low;
    all day long I go about mourning.
My back is filled with searing pain;
    there is no health in my body.
I am feeble and utterly crushed;
    I groan in anguish of heart.
All my longings lie open before you, O LORD;
    my sighing is not hidden from you.
My heart pounds, my strength fails me;
    even the light has gone from my eyes.
My friends and companions avoid me because of my wounds;
    my neighbors stay far away.
Those who seek my life set their traps,
    those who would harm me talk of my ruin;
    all day long they plot deception.
I am like a deaf man, who cannot hear,
    like a mute, who cannot open his mouth;
I have become like a man who does not hear,
    whose mouth can offer no reply.
I wait for you, O LORD;
    you will answer, O Lord my God.
For I said, "Do not let them gloat
    or exalt themselves over me when my foot slips."
For I am about to fall,
    and my pain is ever with me.
I confess my iniquity;
    I am troubled by my sin.
Many are those who are my vigorous enemies;
    those who hate me without reason are numerous.
Those who repay my good with evil
    slander me when I pursue what is good.

O LORD, do not forsake me;
> be not far from me, O my God.
Come quickly to help me,
> O Lord my Savior.

Now let's title it "The Cry of an AIDS Victim." Notice verses 11 and 12: "My friends and companions avoid me because of my wounds; my neighbors stay far away. Those who seek my life set their traps, those who would harm me talk of my ruin; all day long they plot deception."

The plague victim cries out, even willing to confess both sinfulness and stupidity (vv. 3-5, 18), but also reacting to the mean-spiritedness of the age (vv. 11-12, 19-20). Yes, he has a skin disease (vv. 3, 5, 7), but he also has a troubled heart (8, 10) and the inability to communicate his true feelings and respond to others (13, 14). He is alone, suffering from the abandonment of family and friends. So he offers a very personal prayer of lament. His only hope is the Lord.

Who Is to Blame for Urban Migration?

Between January 1525 and 1527 such Anabaptist leaders as George Blaurock stood before the Zurich city council, which eventually banished or drowned them. They refused to go voluntarily, citing Psalm 24, "The earth is the Lord's."[5] That is foundational thinking for what I call a "theology of place."

Then again, read the newspaper, as I did today, and find yet another article about illegal immigrants and migrants crossing borders and wending their way into the cities on all six continents. Now read Psalm 107:1-9.

Give thanks to the LORD, for he is good;
> his love endures forever.
Let the redeemed of the LORD say this—
> those he redeemed from the hand of the foe,
those he gathered from the lands,
> from east and west, from north and south.

Some wandered in desert wastelands,
   finding no way to a city where they could settle.
They were hungry and thirsty,
   and their lives ebbed away.
Then they cried out to the LORD in their trouble,
   and he delivered them from their distress.
He led them by a straight way
   to a city where they could settle.
Let them give thanks to the LORD for his unfailing love
   and his wonderful deeds for men,
for he satisfies the thirsty
   and fills the hungry with good things.

It would appear that if you want to blame someone for the exodus of rural peoples to our cities, you have to blame God for answering the prayers of many people.

For two thousand years the church has had the Great Commission to "go and make disciples of all nations" (Mt 28:19). Today we know where "all the nations" are—in the urban neighborhoods. The frontier of world mission is no longer geographically distant; it's culturally distant but geographically right next door. So, while many may have prayed, "God bless the foreigners—and keep them there," according to the psalmist God is so merciful and so good that he choreographs urban migration. There are so many biblical texts that mess with my narrow class bias and patriotism. This is one of them.

I know it is commonly thought that rural areas or small towns are more hospitable to persons in need than cities are, but my observations convince me that this belief has little basis in fact, either in the Bible or in present-day society.

Clearly Psalm 107 offered hope to the exiled Babylonian refugees. It was probably composed upon their return. The climactic goal of these troubled and harassed people is to turn a desert into a city, with God's help, for dwelling and blessing (vv. 33-40).

That's the biblical picture. I sometimes say with tongue in cheek that Job lived in a rural place and all of his kids died "down on the farm." The Bible doesn't glamorize rural or small-town places.

You've read my reference to Alexander Callow's *American Urban History*,[6] which begins with opening essays contrasting Boston, the public city, and Philadelphia, the private city. Boston was built on the hill to be a light of the gospel, modeling the superior community of the faithful in the wilderness. Philadelphia, by contrast, was a Quaker city that developed from a more privatized, personal spirituality. I muse with the author that it's probably not an accident that Philadelphia became an insurance capital.

Again, the Callow thesis is that these public and private themes became intertwined in American culture. Cities, more than smaller communities, became the places of refuge for most (Mormons were an obvious exception). It's not an accident that the care-giving institutions are set up in our cities. Our "common-grace" public theology as late as the nineteenth and early twentieth centuries demanded that cities respond with a panoply of social reforms and responses to the needy.

There is not time or space for commentary on all of the wisdom texts, but of the following I testify. When our third child died at birth and I wrestled with the why questions, Job comforted me. And when Doris, one of my urban parishioners, lost seven children due to a faulty chimney, resulting in their asphyxiation in one night—the devastating consequence of a landlord's negligence—I immersed myself in Job once again.

The Song of Songs, Ecclesiastes, Proverbs

Leroy Waterman and others helped me see the Song of Songs as a drama[7] (whether of two or three characters scholars disagree), but I took it as a reminder to urban kids to watch out for guys who come on too strong, making all sorts of promises. We shouldn't spiritualize the story away. Urban kids need it, because many of them have engaged in sexual experimentation as children. It may appear to be R-rated to some, but it's a beautiful alternative to the "sex-is-for-sale" culture of our streets.

And if the Song is what urban kids ought to know about sex, Ecclesiastes might be called what urban kids ought to know about education, namely, the limits of Renaissance, values-driven, liberal arts education. Under examination, this kind of education has severe limitations. It needs the outside perspective of a revealed God who enters history and gives us a different perspective on the data of science and philosophy.

Proverbs balances attitudes and actions; private faith and public application in the marketplace of daily life. Abuses and vices are confronted directly (even alcohol, in 23:29-35), as are laziness and a host of lifestyle issues city kids can understand.

The fastest-growing sector of the urban poor in the 1990s are women with children. Most of the families in my last pastorate were female heads of households. For them, Proverbs 31 presents a remarkable example of a virtuous woman who balances her family work, community work and career. Thank God for all the practical and wonderfully diverse models of family and community in the urban Bible.

Lament for the City

Finally, a chapter on "urban poets" would not be complete without looking at the Book of Lamentations. Lamentations can be subtitled "A Funeral for a City," for the entire book is a dirge. As I read this book, I feel I'm being taken on a city tour. My guide loves this old city in all its parts. Furthermore, he has poetically arranged his laments into an acrostic. Each verse is built on one of the twenty-two letters of the Hebrew alphabet.

The public squares are nearly empty now (1:1). Gloom sweeps like fog through the streets. Why is this happening? Count the reasons in chapter 2, beginning with the anger of Almighty God.

The worst of it is that the city had been warned for centuries, and now the promise has come true (2:17). Images of holocausts gone by come to mind as we pass by the piles of bodies in the streets.

The walking metaphor continues in chapter 3. I think our tour guide is alone now, trying to comprehend what he's seen. The death of the city has left him so exposed, vulnerable and afraid. I think it has dawned on him how much of his own identity and security was wrapped up in that vibrant world-class city.

Then, when he is nearly overcome with despair, suddenly he hears a song in the distance. Hope is stirred again (3:20), and he moves closer and hears the choir singing:

Great is Thy faithfulness! Great is Thy faithfulness!

Morning by morning new mercies I see.

All I have needed Thy hand hath provided.

Great is Thy faithfulness, Lord, unto me!

You don't see the choir mentioned in the text? Come on, it's poetry, remember. One thing I think we know for sure is where Thomas O. Chisholm was having his devotions in 1923 when he borrowed the words of Lamentations for his beloved poem that we still sing as a hymn.

The good news of the gospel is that the Lord God will always hear those who pray in faith:

The LORD is good to those whose hope is in him,

    to the one who seeks him;

it is good to wait quietly

    for the salvation of the LORD. (Lam 3:25-26)

I can't tell you how many times I sang "Great Is Thy Faithfulness" before I realized it's not a promise for me only; it is for all those trapped in the ruins of a thousand Beiruts, Sarajevos or Belfasts. It's a promise to all city dwellers. Never lose hope.

With new hope our Lamentations guide returns to public ministry in the city. He identifies himself with all the citizens and cries out in prayers on behalf of the whole city.

> Let us examine our ways and test them,
>> and let us return to the LORD.
> Let us lift up our hearts and our hands
>> to God in heaven, and say:
> "We have sinned and rebelled
>> and you have not forgiven." (3:40-42)

Chapters 4 and 5 continue the lament. Much of it is historical reflection with contemporary application. It concludes with contrasting observations:

About God:

> You, O LORD, reign forever;
>> your throne endures from generation to generation. (5:19)

About the city:

> Why do you always forget us?
>> Why do you forsake us so long?
> Restore us to yourself, O LORD, that we may return;
>> renew our days as of old. (5:20-21)

It's as though the city has become a cemetery and we are all there. Unless God intervenes, the city will not live again. Corporate judgment is no fairy tale.

It is very dark. There is one last cry:

> . . . unless you have utterly rejected us
>> and are angry with us beyond measure. (5:22)

The curtain falls; the funeral is over.

8
WHAT CITIES OUGHT TO LOOK LIKE
ISAIAH'S VISION

Your people will rebuild the ancient ruins
and will raise up the age-old foundations;
you will be called Repairer of Broken Walls,
Restorer of Streets with Dwellings.
Isaiah 58:12

THE OPENING VISION OF ISAIAH is one of cities on fire (1:7). Burning cities in Judah were intended as a wake-up call for Judah. As far as we know, Isaiah's entire career was as an urban prophet. He uses the word *city* nearly sixty times, and for him cities came to symbolize nations. Clearly, this book reveals an urban perspective. In fact, I'd go beyond that to say Isaiah was an urban person with a global worldview. He saw God's transcendence (chap. 6) over Judah's empty national throne, and his lens on all of life was thereby affected.

This book paints cities in varied colors. Consider, for example, the predicted plunder and rape of Zion (3:1-7). Contrast that with the metaphor of the superhighway linking Assyria (now Iraq), Israel and Egypt (19:23-25). It was no narrow nationalist who said, "The LORD Almighty will bless them, saying, 'Blessed be Egypt my people, Assyria my handiwork, and Israel my inheritance.' "

Isaiah could see the day when three enemy nations would be reconciled and linked by divine intervention.

Comfort for the Cities

If Isaiah 1—39 provides a theology of the city, chapters 40—66 provide a theology *for* the city. The theme shifts from judgment to comfort, and I like to think of this entire section as the theological rationale for the rebuilding of Jerusalem.

Babylon has fallen, Persia reigns and Cyrus the Persian is viewed as "my servant," God's person who let the people go back to their land after years of captivity (45:1).

We are familiar with this phenomenon. Was Gorbachev "God's servant," as many believe, who allowed the "openness and restructuring" (*glasnost* and *peristroika*) that led to the dismantling of the Soviet Empire in 1990? Was Minister Farakhan of the Nation of Islam God's servant with his idea for the "Million Man March" on Washington in 1995, as many others believe? (According to some reports, 61 percent of the men marching were professing Christians.)

A reading of Isaiah from an urban vantage point illustrates how common it has been among Christians to read from a rural perspective. Consider this quote:

How beautiful on the mountains
  are the feet of those who bring good news,
who proclaim peace,
  who bring good tidings,
  who proclaim salvation,
who say to Zion,
  "Your God reigns!" (52:7)

So often we use this text to talk about going to faraway missionary jungles.

Wrong. This is an urban evangelist's text. It talks about proclaiming the good news to Zion. If the city is reached, the ends of the earth (v. 10) will hear about it.

A Worldwide Vision

Isaiah has profoundly altered my own ministry over the years by providing both a missiology of the city and a theology for the city. Let me explain briefly.

. The four Servant Songs in 40—66, including the best-known in chapter 53, place the redeemed city in the context of world redemption. I agree with the late David Bosch, who argues that Paul's eschatologically driven mission is to go beyond Rome, the world's capital city, to Tarshish (ancient Spain).[1] (See Rom 15:24; compare Is 66:18-20.)

The Isaiah vision is never exclusively local. The biblical city is the place of redeemed nations, not only in heaven (Rev 21) but also on earth. Isaiah and Paul knew, as Christ did, that Israel's God was no tribal god.

For nearly twenty years I have been in conflict with some urban ministry colleagues precisely over this issue. As a white male in America, I've been accused of using this global mission vision to avoid dealing with the African-American community and its aspirations (propelling my urban commitment worldwide while neglecting the horrors of urban racism here in the United States). Some urban Christians are profoundly antimissionary, and I must confess they have some very good reasons to feel this way. This is a tension I take very seriously as I consider my own ministry.

When American missionaries who have never set foot in our American cities cross oceans at great financial cost to tell Africans, Asians or Latins how to do urban ministry, it is an affront to me also. The issue is not new. Remember my prior reference to 1890 when the Victorian mission hero Henry M. Stanley (of Livingstone fame) published his "white man's burden" text, *In Darkest Africa: The Way In*,[2] to which an affronted William Booth (of Salvation Army fame) published his response, *In Darkest England: The Way Out*.[3]

Pastor and Chaplain

Personally, I am committed to the vision of a local church and its pastors with two basic functions: pastor to the faithful and chaplain to the whole community. There is an obvious tension between the incarnation of Jesus and the necessary localisms of ministry in Jesus' name. Theologically Jesus Christ was totally and profoundly local. Yet he is also the ascended, cosmic Christ. It took the church 125 years, from Nicea to Chalcedon (A.D. 325-451), to decide how the two natures of Christ could be described. As I will show in my chapter on Ezekiel, the biblical view of city is not exclusively local. It never was.

Like Christ, Christ's followers are multidimensional people. I am *in* Christ while I am *at* Chicago. Like Augustine, I affirm the past as a present memory and the future as a present possibility. I'm never completely at home anyplace or anytime on earth.

The deeper I go into the city of Chicago where I've lived and served, the more clearly I see the blood lines of our people traced back to Poland, to Ireland, to Korea, to El Salvador, to Mississippi, to West Africa. Isaiah helps me with the concept of transcendence. The whole city, not my people or my neighborhood alone, is to be the focus of ministry.

A Social Vision

Isaiah also provides a theology for the city by providing a social vision in texts like 65:17-25:

"Behold, I will create
    new heavens and a new earth.
The former things will not be remembered,
    nor will they come to mind.
But be glad and rejoice forever
    in what I will create,
for I will create Jerusalem to be a delight
    and its people a joy.
I will rejoice over Jerusalem
    and take delight in my people;
the sound of weeping and of crying

will be heard in it no more.
"Never again will there be in it
   an infant who lives but a few days,
     or an old man who does not live out his years;
he who dies at a hundred
   will be thought a mere youth;
he who fails to reach a hundred
   will be considered accursed.
They will build houses and dwell in them;
   they will plant vineyards and eat their fruit.
No longer will they build houses and others live in them,
   or plant and others eat.
For as the days of a tree,
   so will be the days of my people;
my chosen ones will long enjoy
   the works of their hands.
They will not toil in vain
   or bear children doomed to misfortune;
for they will be a people blessed by the LORD,
   they and their descendants with them.
Before they call I will answer;
   while they are still speaking I will hear.
The wolf and the lamb will feed together,
   and the lion will eat straw like the ox,
   but dust will be the serpent's food.
They will neither harm nor destroy
   on all my holy mountain," says the LORD.

Remember, this was intended to be an encouragement to urban builders on their way back to renovate Jerusalem. God reminds them (and us) that the eternal city is also under construction. We will live there forever as believers.

And what are the key components of the city God is building?

☐ Public celebrations and happiness (vv. 17-25)

- ☐ Public health for children and aged (v. 20)
- ☐ Housing for all (v. 21)
- ☐ Food for all (v. 22)
- ☐ Family support systems (v. 23)
- ☐ Absence of violence (v. 25)

Put simply, if this is what God says a city ought to look like, and if God's Spirit lives in me, this is what I want Chicago to look like. For me, it's not enough to measure growing churches in the city. This text forces me to look also at the social side effects of churches filled with urban disciples of Jesus.

Obviously, this perspective gets me in trouble with some colleagues and friends who agree with the idea of a missiology of the city but haven't also affirmed a theology for that same city.

When the gifted evangelist John Dawson wrote *Taking Our Cities for Christ*,[4] I celebrated the attention given to the spiritual side of work in urban ministry, including taking on Satan's strongholds. In all candor, however, two things were missing for me in the book. First, the city church was absent. The "taking" would be done from outside the city. Second, the "taking" metaphor absolutizes the so-called "stronghold" texts of Scripture and tends to gloss over or ignore the social vision passages, the four hundred texts on the poor in the Bible and the sixty-three of them that call for urban justice.

The way I talk about integrating these positions might become clearer when I contrast the public faith of Colossians with the private faith of Philippians later in this book.

I conclude by saying Isaiah never gives me permission to see the so-called inner city as having preference over the outer city or suburbs. Cities are viewed as a whole, not only socially but historically. Isaiah gives the long view of redemption.

9
JEREMIAH'S LETTER TO URBAN FAMILIES
(& DANIEL'S RESPONSE)

Also, seek the peace and prosperity
of the city to which I have carried you
into exile. Pray to the LORD for it,
because if it prospers, you too will prosper.
Jeremiah 29:7

JEREMIAH'S LETTER TO THE EXILES who had been forcibly relocated in Babylon by Nebuchadnezzar, the three-time destroyer of Jerusalem, impacted me and many of my colleagues when we read George Webber's exposition of the text in *God's Colony in Man's World.*[1] Webber represented a community-based movement known as East Harlem Protestant Parish that began producing a lot of helpful literature about the time I entered Chicago as an assistant pastor and seminary student in 1965 after six years of ministry in Seattle.

Jeremiah's letter, preserved in chapter 29 of the book of Jeremiah, does not appear out of the blue sky. Earlier the prophet, who lived through the sieges Isaiah predicted, borrowed language similar to Isaiah's. Nebuchadnezzar is pictured as God's servant (Jer 25:9; 27:6). For Isaiah, Cyrus was shepherd and servant (Is 44:28; 45:1).

These are theological reflections by Spirit-led people on the great events of their own days. Obviously both prophets believed God had many nonconventional ways of accomplishing world redemption.

Exiles Are Shown the Bigger Picture

So, while everyone else viewed the destruction of Jerusalem and its temple as the tragic conclusion, Jeremiah saw something else. While the Jews grumbled in their Babylonian ghettos a thousand miles from Jerusalem, wallowing as victims in their own hopelessness, the prophet proclaimed a bigger picture.

The letter was doubtless read in a strong voice to crowds in the street struggling to hear the written text read aloud. Notice several points in this letter.

1. The God of Israel is quoted as speaking "to all those I carried into exile from Jerusalem to Babylon" (Jer 29:4). Can't you hear the first murmurs of the crowd? *What was that pronoun? What do you mean, "those I carried"? Nebuchadnezzar dragged me over here.*

Viewed theologically, these exiles were not victims; they were on a mission from God. Dare I say it? I began to realize that I was not a student minister sent to endure Chicago while preparing for ministry elsewhere—I also was *sent* to Chicago.

2. "Build houses and settle down. . . . Marry and have sons and daughters" (vv. 5-6). Refugees naturally keep their most valuable suitcases packed. They don't intend to stay. "And raise your kids there in Babylon." *Bilingual kids? How awful! This is getting worse.*

3. "Also, seek the peace and prosperity of the city to which I have carried you into exile. Pray to the LORD for it, because if it prospers, you too will prosper" (v. 7). *We should help these uncircumcised Babylonians prosper? After what they've done to us?* How unbelievably hard it must have been for those Jewish war victims, forcibly marched from Jerusalem to Babylon, to hear these words. God is not asking the exiles to lead a passive, patient existence in the enemy city. He's asking that they actively work for Babylon's *shalom,* that is, peace with justice. Moreover, the promise is that they and presumably their families will be blessed thereby.

Could it be, I asked in 1965, that God was asking me to seek the *shalom* of Chicago, this dirty, ugly, flat, corrupt city? Could I believe that if I truly did so, God would bless my own family with true *shalom?* I must tell you, raising my kids in inner-city Chicago was totally off my map of life's expectations.

This text rearranged my priorities. I was preparing my mind to go to Yale and be a pastor in a "successful" church, like most of my colleagues. I had read a lot of missionary biographies over the years; I knew God expected missionaries to expose their kids to dangers. But pastors' kids were exempt, right? It took Corean and me more than a year to sort through these issues.

I didn't see how I could pastor poor people and not have our kids go to school with them, so we committed our kids to public schools. With three sons, we experienced about thirty-two years in these schools. Frankly, I concluded if God were calling us, our kids were included.[2] We stopped apologizing for where and how we lived. I don't want to imply it was easy for them; my kids all struggled with growing and learning in a chaotic and even violent environment. Now, as adults, I think they can appreciate how their early years, including their school experience, were used by God. In fact, our youngest son, Brian, who as a young man forsook the inner city, has been called back to the very Uptown community where he grew up. He is now on the staff at Uptown Baptist Church involved in creative art ministry. Ironically, he is also a director of the church's community outreach programs—the very community he wanted no part of.

4. "When seventy years are completed for Babylon, I will come to you and fulfill my gracious promise to bring you back to this place" (v. 10).

In retrospect, we can see that God was using the Babylonian exile to teach Israel profound truths with enormous mission significance.

From this point on, the people of Israel would be called "Jews" and would learn skills that would make them successful in every urban setting. Babylon was their graduate school. Furthermore, without the Temple and the *shekinah* glory (that living presence of the Holy God), and without a professional priesthood, Israel's theology and ministry practices would undergo a radical transformation. Judaism would become crossculturally adaptive, and Jews would speak many languages.

"Mission is the mother of theology," wrote Martin Kahler in 1909, and so it is. In exile, the Jews were forced to be bilingual; they developed the synagogue; they recovered the doctrine of angels as globally significant ministering spirits (see Dan 9), a doctrine virtually unneeded and unheeded back in Jerusalem.

So the synagogue with its empowered laity was a gift of the exile. To borrow contemporary language, the institutions of Jerusalem were "reinvented." G. F. Moore, a marvelous scholar whose essay on first-century Judaism I encountered back in 1968, called Judaism "a veritable flower garden of religious pluralism."[2]

Daniel Practices Jeremiah's Theology

Daniel too lived through the captivity in exile, serving as a lay prophet in a so-called pagan government for his entire adult life. For me, he is an example of one who most obviously lived out Jeremiah's challenge to seek the *shalom* of the city.

The details are familiar to the children of Bible believers. I was raised on Daniel stories. Never, though, can I remember hearing the story told to motivate and guide Christians to serve in pagan governmental structures.

Daniel's secret seems to have come to him early in his palace schooling. Somehow, this kid (the text indicates that he and his friends were *naharim,* or teenagers) sorted out faith and culture issues at an early age. He mastered the Babylonian wisdom tradition, while rejecting some Babylonian values.

When I served as youth and music director in my first church back in Seattle, Daniel became my model for urban Christian education. I thought we should expose kids to the best the world has to offer and not always hide the worst (that usually backfires) but always teach biblical virtues and appeal to discernment.

No matter how you look at it, Daniel's commitment to making the Babylon government more just for all the people may have prolonged the empire. Who do you think ran the government while Nebuchadnezzar was out of his mind for seven years? (4:32).

I can't resist reminding Americans during the past decade that God called such Jewish leaders as Daniel to serve in the governments of the land we today know as Iraq (Babylon) and Iran (Persia). Do you suppose these leaders prayed for their "adopted" lands? Of course.

Here's a stretch for you. Suppose their prayers are still being heard by an eternal God. Do you think that makes a difference in how we should view Saddam Hussein of Iraq or the Ayatollah of Iran?

Think about it!

10
THINKING BIBLICALLY
ABOUT THE FAMILY
(WITH THE HELP OF EZEKIEL)

And say, "This is what the Sovereign LORD *says*
to Jerusalem: Your ancestry and birth
were in the land of the Canaanites;
your father was an Amorite and your mother
a Hittite. . . . Your older sister was Samaria,
who lived to the north of you with her daughters;
and your younger sister, who lived to the south
of you with her daughters, was Sodom."
Ezekiel 16:3, 46

THE PROMOTION OF "FAMILY VALUES" is a major growth industry in our time. Newspapers, talk radio, journals and seminars provide a steady stream of ideas to strengthen families. As a pastor and a parent, I can attest to the need for lots of help in this area.

I have concluded that the concept of family is much more elastic in Scripture than we might expect. The classic text which brings the twin themes of family and city together is the whole chapter of Ezekiel 16.

This text is addressed to Jerusalem with this remarkable introduction: "Your ancestry and birth were in the land of the Canaanites; your father was an Amorite and your mother a Hittite" (v. 3). Right away we observe that for Ezekiel ethnicity flows seamlessly into geography, and to make the "patriots" nervous, God suggests that from the beginning until now Jerusalem has been a mixed-racial city. That mixed-racial community has become family. Images of ethnic superiority are dashed at the outset. Moreover, they are adopted family (vv. 6-7). Israel wasn't a great nation because of its racial and ethnic purity. Just the opposite was true. It was from the unwanted of other nations that God formed the people who lived in Jerusalem. God made them beautiful and great. (I think of George Bernard Shaw's *Pygmalion* or "My Fair Lady.")

Now let's skip over the historical and judgment narratives to verses 44–47:

> Everyone who quotes proverbs will quote this proverb about you: "Like mother, like daughter." You are a true daughter of your mother, who despised her husband and her children; and you are a true sister of your sisters, who despised their husbands and their children. Your mother was a Hittite and your father an Amorite. Your older sister was Samaria, who lived to the north of you with her daughters; and your younger sister, who lived to the south of you with her daughters, was Sodom. You not only walked in their ways and copied their detestable practices, but in all your ways you soon became more depraved than they.

Here now is our family systems diagram taken from the biblical perspective (see figure 1).

The city as seen from God's perspective now takes shape as a family system, and everyone today should know how significant family systems are. Regional cities are sisters and suburbs are daughters in God's kingdom perspective.

And so I set about to map my city, Chicago, from this perspective—a small diagonal cut of Chicago seen as family (see figure 2).

In fact, Chicago shares a common water system with Milwaukee, ninety miles north, and a common water and sewer system with our southern sisters—sewer system because since 1906 we've pumped sewage into the rivers that affect these sister cities.

A Responsible Family

Forgive my simplicity at this point, but if you trace all the family migrant streams to Chicago, earlier from Europe and now from Latin America, Africa and the Middle East, there is really no such

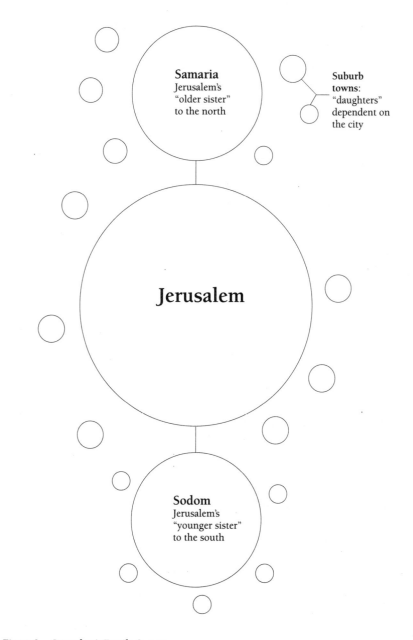

Figure 1.   Jerusalem's Family System

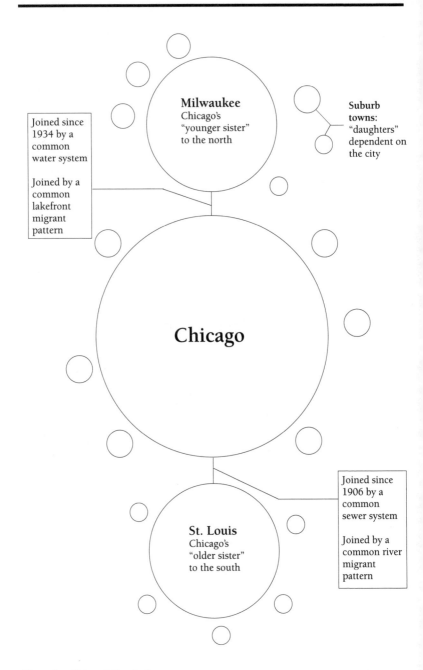

Milwaukee
Chicago's
"younger sister"
to the north

Suburb
towns:
"daughters"
dependent on
the city

Joined since
1934 by a
common
water system

Joined by a
common
lakefront
migrant
pattern

Chicago

Joined since
1906 by a
common
sewer system

Joined by a
common river
migrant
pattern

St. Louis
Chicago's
"older sister"
to the south

Figure 2. Chicago's Family System

place as "away" anymore.

Moreover, if suburbs are children of the city, I cannot discount them in family thinking or service provisions. My map expands. So much for "them versus us" thinking. The only appropriate view of the city is both metropolitan and international.

Ezekiel's map helps me address the environmental issues of resource scarcity (water, land and so on) and toxic-waste displacement. If other distant cities and nearby small towns are family, we wouldn't want to dump all our incinerators into one family's community, would we?

So if my state, which has 102 counties, gangs up on Chicago, which is largely one county, that's not fair either, is it? And if the schools for one part of the family are highly developed and well funded, but other members of the family are left with perpetually bad schools, that's not right, is it? Psalm 24:1 reminds us, "The earth is the LORD's." Ezekiel 16 helps us see some of the very concrete implications of such audacious theological thinking.

If my government's policies perpetually provide tax incentives for companies many miles from job holders, again the fairness issue arises. If the government increases its 90 percent share of interstate expressway costs while simultaneously reducing its share of city mass-transit costs, is not that raising the family fairness issues?

I think God is calling us to encourage and call all Christian believers to work in the public arena on issues exactly like these. This too is part of a metropolitan spirituality, and it has been neglected far too long by people who claim to be biblical.

Now, as if this has not been radical or traumatic enough for most Western Christians, Ezekiel decides to illustrate his point by a specific reference to Sodom.

Why exactly did God destroy Sodom? Ezekiel provides the divine insight on Genesis 18 and 19 when he quotes God as saying, "Now this was the sin of your sister Sodom: She and her daughters were arrogant, overfed and unconcerned; they did not help the poor and needy. They were haughty and did detestable things before me. Therefore I did away with them as you have seen" (Ezek 16:49-50).

What then was the terrible sin of Sodom that caused God to destroy it?

She (the city) and her daughters (suburbs) had a surplus of wealth, pride and lust; she didn't care for the poor and needy.

I ask again: Do you know of any city in the world today where the rich are getting richer and the poor are getting poorer? There's no city where the gap between rich and poor is *not* widening. This was the Sodom disease.

Put candidly, when either the children of the city (suburbs) or the city itself abdicates its *mutual* responsibility, it's a very grave situation, precisely because of the theological principles established in this chapter. Cities, suburbs and migrant streams are *family!*

If I'm reading this text and my context correctly, America is in grave danger for what we're doing to huge sectors of our family.

Some of the oldest churches in Christendom, the Middle-Eastern Orthodox family of churches, are among our newest neighbors in Western cities. At a time when Islam is growing rapidly all over the world, God seems to be scattering the very Christians who have lived with Muslims since the sixth century. These new neighbors, often bearded in black robes with large crosses, have lived with Muslims since the time of John of Damascus in the seventh century. They've forgotten more about Islam than we Westerners will ever know.

Isn't it amazingly gracious of our God to bring our ancient Christian leaders to be side by side with us in Western cities on the eve of the third millennium? No doubt, while they come to renew us, God may use us to encourage, strengthen and renew them. We are family! It's in our cities that we experience it first.

11
MAJOR THEMES IN MINOR PROPHETS

He has showed you, O man, what is good.
And what does the LORD require of you?
To act justly and to love mercy
and to walk humbly with your God.
Listen! The LORD is calling to the city.
Micah 6:8-9

MANY TIMES OVER THE YEARS I've sat down and read the twelve minor prophets in a single sitting. I find it emotionally exhilarating and numbing at the same time.

The urban-versus-rural themes loom always. The prostitute theme of Hosea is urban; the locust plagues of Joel are rural. (Perhaps we urban types could more easily identify with a bubonic plague carried by rats and fleas.) Amos and Haggai evoke contrasting perspectives on urban worship centers. Haggai builds one, and Amos comes off the farm to rail against another.

Habakkuk is the urban version of the Job story. Not only do righteous people suffer for no just cause, but apparently very evil cities can be used by God to discipline what appear to be less evil cities.

Zephaniah provides hope for God's ultimate justice for all urban refugees, while Micah provides a summary of what I call "Capital City Spirituality":

What does the LORD require of you?
To act justly and to love mercy
    and to walk humbly with your God.
Listen! The LORD is calling to the city—
    and to fear your name is wisdom—
    "Heed the rod and the One who appointed it." (Mic 6:8-9)
To act justly requires a balance of theory and action on behalf of
others.

To love mercy requires a continual dependence on God's forgiveness and grace.

To walk humbly with God implies a constant dependence on resources beyond our own.

So many who have quoted this text in my hearing over the years have failed to point out the context where this balanced spirituality is to be lived out. See verse 9 for the phrase "to the city." This is not a private faith. Its intention is for the public square of engagement in the city.

Malachi reviews a potpourri of subjects from spiritual complacency (chap. 1) and corrupt clergy (chap. 2) to messages about divorce and tithing, and concludes with the prediction that the Messiah or "Son of Righteousness" will come in the future (chap. 4).

Let's return at this point to three profoundly urban writings among the twelve: Obadiah, Jonah and Nahum.

Obadiah

Obadiah is a classic "tale of two cities" drama. This drama in the shortest book in the Old Testament plays out over many centuries. In fact, the conflict of Jacob and Esau in Genesis had mushroomed to become a quarrel among nations of their descendants with Jerusalem and Petra respectively as their capitals.

The drama has five acts:

Act I Jacob and Esau act out their sibling rivalry (Gen 25; 27).

Act II Edom (Esau's descendants) denies highway access to Moses

(Jacob's descendants) (Num 20:14).

Act III Israel strikes back under Saul (1 Sam 14) and David (2 Sam 8:13; 1 Kings 11), and Solomon encroaches on Edom (1 Kings 9:26).

Act IV Petra celebrates Jerusalem's defeat (see Ps 137:7; Obad 12).

Act V Petra rules Jerusalem. As bizarre as this sounds, it's true. The Edomites were forced into the southeast corner of Jerusalem. One of the Idumean descendants was Herod the Great, whose family ruled Jerusalem until the Roman conquest in A.D. 70. Obadiah ends with the promise that someday the kingdom shall be the Lord's.

How does this little history book shape a Christian worldview? By emphasizing the following principles:

☐ Quarrels among nations are ultimately quarrels among brothers.

☐ Foreign policy is a legitimate Christian concern. Nations generally act out of perceived national interests, but limits are needed. There is also an implied golden rule to "treat other nations the way you would wish your nation to be treated."

☐ Neutrality in the face of oppression will be judged. Edom should not have turned its back on the cries for help from Jerusalem.

☐ Beware of dependence on geopolitical security. Petra's fortress could withstand everything, as it turned out, except a new trade route that circumvented it. The United States has been magnificently shielded by huge oceans from many of the world's conflicts. Chicago survived the transition from rail center to world's largest airport, but we must beware of placing security in such external phenomena.

Because God in Christ entered history in real time and space, the followers of Jesus take history and geography very seriously. Obadiah is a model of reading the city from a theological vantage point.

Jonah

Jonah and Nahum, taken together, form a historical parenthesis around Nineveh and God's dealings with what was arguably the most violent city in the ancient Near East. The hero of the Jonah story is not the prophet or the fish, but the struggle of the Almighty God to get a message of grace and forgiveness to the capital of the Assyrian Empire.

Many of the several thousand books in my library have special meaning, but one about Jonah always brings a smile. I found this little nineteenth-century book, *Patriot & Revivalist,* written by an Englishman named F. S. Webster.[1] For him Jonah's problem was his patriotism. I describe it as "wrapping the gospel in his flag." Jonah assumed his enemies were also God's enemies. Jonah was a cultural chauvinist and an ethnocentrist. He had very good reasons for not loving Assyrians, considering all they had done and would continue to do to Israel over hundreds of years, including taking the northern tribes into captivity.

So, Jonah "bought the one-way ticket, but God gave him the round trip." Nineveh was east; he went west. I can understand this. Suppose God called a New York Jewish businessman and said, "Weinstein, go to Berlin and preach the gospel. I'll reward your ministry and make Germany greater than it was under Hitler." Sure, I can understand Jonah's reluctance. There are a few cities, and a few places in my own city, that I'd be reluctant to visit, let alone preach in.

The story is wonderful. We witness an ecumenical prayer meeting on the ship and a compassionate crew that throws the prophet overboard in a last-ditch attempt to save themselves. We see their concession to God at his demise (1:16). Longtime Pittsburgh preacher Clarence Macartney titled the second chapter of his book *Strange Texts: Grand Truths* "A Whale's Belly for a Pulpit," but I see what Jonah did in there more as a prayer meeting.[2] Then there's more action. I like the vividness of the verb in 2:10, "vomit." Can't you see the urban prophet lying in the vomit of a sick fish on the beach?

Jonah preaches to the city after his second-chance call in chapter 3, but he preaches only half the gospel: "Repent! You're going to hell in forty days!" He's orthodox, but he fails altogether to communicate God's heartbeat of concern and mercy.

Finally, he's on the hill on the thirty-ninth day, probably having his devotional from Genesis 18 (praying something like "Lord, you destroyed Sodom once—I believe you can do it again!"). Instead, the God who made the big fish in chapter 1 makes the little worm in chapter 4 that destroys Jonah's shady observation post.

He's devastated and pouts at the greatest revival before Pentecost. The truth that he'll live with Assyrians in heaven forever hasn't sunk in yet. He can't handle it.

God speaks. The book ends with a question to Jonah: "Shouldn't I care about 120,000 (babies) who don't know their right hand from the left and much cattle?"

Cattle? Why care about cattle? This is a Middle-Eastern word picture. It was a cattle culture. Cattle are synonymous for wealth. So God is saying, "Shouldn't I care about the children and the economy of this great city?"

There are questions we still must ask, of course. How did this little book get into the Bible anyway? Is it a true story? Here's the explanation I love from my little book *Patriot & Revivalist:* "To invent incidents which no one believes, in order to enforce lessons which no one wishes to learn, seems the height of absurdity."[3] It's too contrary. It must be true.

What a surprise. I pick up Nahum, written a century later, and find the prophet saying, "Woe to the city of blood (Nineveh)." Nineveh, the city of revival in Jonah's day, will now be a city judged—and executed, as it turns out, by the Babylonians in 612 B.C.

So the revival vanished without a historical trace, meaning for many that Jonah was a nonhistorical story. The late Harvard professor William McLoughlin's study of the religious awakenings in American history[4] points out that true revival has profound social consequences. Timothy Smith's *Revivalism and Social Reform*[5] and Norris Magnuson's *Salvation in the Slums*[6] make the same point.

Jonah preached half the gospel—a scare tactic, if you please. Revival without discipleship is a dangerous thing. I think about this when I read that we have forty or fifty million Christians in American churches on Sunday—at least 65,000 black churches alone—and yet see how little the impact is on many issues of consequence. Do I think that America's spirituality could vanish without a trace over a one-hundred-year period? Please don't ask; my response may depress you. I remember Nineveh.

Obviously there is a legitimate critique of the evangelism in the Jonah story. This side of Pentecost we should know and do better in declaring and demonstrating the gospel by word, by deed and, if God blesses, by signs that follow. But the Jonah story should cause us to adjust our maps and take the gospel beyond the safety of our class and race. The whole gospel for the whole city is what's required.

12
WHEN ALL ELSE FAILS, SEND THE CHOIR
REFLECTIONS ON CHRONICLES

After consulting the people, Jehoshaphat appointed
men to sing to the LORD and to praise him for
the splendor of his holiness as they went out
at the head of the army, saying:
"Give thanks to the LORD,
for his love endures forever."
2 Chronicles 20:21

I'VE DONE A FAIR AMOUNT of research and reflection on Samuel, Kings and Chronicles over the years. Both Samuel and Kings are political histories written from a strongly empirical point of view. Let's call it the palace perspective. Of necessity, these books are city texts, full of civics lessons, culminating with dramatic but practical lessons on strategies for the capture of a city in the ancient world (2 Kings 25).

In contrast, I believe the books called Chronicles emerged from documents compiled by folks combing through the ruins of destroyed cities after the captivity and exile in Babylon. The events depicted in Chronicles are from the same time period as Samuel and Kings, but they represent a theological perspective not originating in the palace. In Chronicles Israel is viewed as a theocracy. David and Solomon are idealized, and the message is: Here's how the Lord meets all needs, both material and spiritual.

History from a New Perspective

In the Chronicles we find an attempt to shape an old history for a new, postexilic generation that is seeking its roots. History is not just a study of the past. Archaeology is a study of the past. History, by contrast, is a study of the written records of the past. I remember very well the way we were taught American history as European descendants here in America. Think of how different Columbus looks today to South and North Americans.

I'm reminded of Henry Steele Commager's startling comment in his *America: The Story of a Free People* that archaeologists a few thousand years from now, when digging through the ruins of twentieth-century barbecues, rusted-out campers and ruined trailer parks, may rightly conclude that the Indians conquered *us*. History is all about perspective.[1]

The Chronicles include palace murders, conspiracies, intrigue, incest and royal adultery in technicolor. These are heroic portraits. Likewise, the temple, rather than the palace, is the focal point. The battle victors are priests, Levite custodians and especially musicians. The court power brokers of 1 and 2 Kings have moved offstage for now. In Chronicles, "faith is the victory," and temple leaders are the real heroes.

In the early-nineties Hollywood movie *Sister Act,* Whoopie Goldberg plays a Las Vegas showgirl who hides from the mob in a city-center convent. In the space of a few weeks she transforms the nuns' choir from a god-awful, "Lord-have-mercy" group to a force that transforms the whole urban neighborhood.

We wish it could be so easy. Since 1990, the United States has sent military troops into Mogadishu, Somalia; Port-au-Prince, Haiti; and, most recently, the cities of Bosnia as part of the accords drafted to bring a cease-fire to the Balkan states of the former Yugoslavia. Personally, I think a powerful nation like the United States must assume the role of urban police in some of the world's most desperate situations. Our troops have occupied the Korean peninsula for nearly fifty years now. The problems just don't go away. Armies have limits. Politics is, after all, the "art of the possible," as city dwellers know well. I believe that the United Nations as well as regional economic and security alliances are necessary and should be encouraged. Collective security is a good idea. But I'm also a realist. There are limits. No system is foolproof. Our only security ultimately is in Jesus!

Remember also, little Israel existed vulnerably in a narrow sliver of land, a land bridge, in fact, that tied three continents together. Humanly speaking, Israel existed by the good pleasure of great powers.

But Israel's spiritual leaders knew they had a God with powers greater than the armies of surrounding nations. So, confronted by 300,000 Ethiopian troops, Asa was forced to pray (2 Chron 14:11). He knew military might could never be the ultimate defense. He was right.

Solomon envisioned a temple that could serve as a worship place for all nations (2 Chron 5—6). What a contrary worldview. Instead of imagining armies going out to conquer nations, he saw migrant streams of foreign pilgrims coming to Jerusalem to encounter and worship the cosmic God (2 Chron 6:18), the God who could be met in a temple in the city. This was the God who promised healing to the land if the people would pray (2 Chron 7:14).

Prayer and Work
Of course, prayers of faith never come alone. Faith always leads to work, and we see that justice in the land requires godly, discerning judicial leaders as well (2 Chron 19:5-7). Godly people take their faith into public engagement, especially in Chronicles.

The reason prayers are required in cities today is the same as in ancient Israel. Satan is intervening in the day-to-day decisions of even our best leaders (1 Chron 21:1). Human explanations aren't enough. The demonic is on the loose in our cities, and in such power and numbers that huge urban populations know full well that a limited left-brain, rational view of our situation cannot account for all of it, nor can such a view deliver us.

So Jehoshaphat's intelligence department briefed him on the desperate situation. Judah was surrounded by a coalition of enemy armies. With spiritual sensitivity and insight, Jehoshaphat first called the people to fast and pray; then he sent an expanded robed choir of Levites, Kohathites and Korahites to the front lines (2 Chron 20:18-23) to sing of God's steadfast love, creating an ambush of confusion. The enemy soldiers killed each other! The victory of the choir in the fields was celebrated by the orchestra back at the temple with harps, lyres and trumpets (20:28).

After thirty-five years of city ministry, I too can testify that urban churches are pulling together their scarce resources to build or renovate church buildings and call the nations to worship. For the nations have come to the city neighborhoods in our time. Against all odds the churches sing, and miracles happen. Kids are reached, families transformed; drug pushers flee, and the Word of God sung and danced by his people puts Satan to flight.

Virtually unarmed and vulnerable, Israel celebrated God's triumph over the armies of Pharaoh with an antiphonal choir and musical celebration in the wilderness (Ex 15). Paul and Silas sang a duet at midnight, and God opened the prison for ministry in Philippi, a significant Roman city (Acts 16).

Personally, I am always amazed and humbled by God's surprising interventions when my academic degrees and long experience are of no help at all. More often than not, the choir is more than adequate.

13
THE PERSIAN PARTNERSHIP FOR THE REBUILDING OF JERUSALEM

They said to me, "Those who survived the exile
and are back in the province are in great trouble
and disgrace. The wall of Jerusalem is broken down,
and its gates have been burned with fire."
Nehemiah 1:3

THE HISTORICAL SECTION OF THE Bible concludes with three books from the Persian Empire, the land we call Iran today. How ironic that Iran and Iraq should have such a central role in the Jewish-Christian Bible.

I believe Ezra, Nehemiah and Esther should be studied together, for they were all working on one problem—the future of Israel. For decades Bible scholars have called the study of the first three Gospels (Matthew, Mark and Luke) the "Synoptic Gospels" because Christ's life can only be seen *(optic)* by taking the Gospels as a whole or "together" *(syn-optic)*.

Similarly, I contend we have here synoptic histories, where two lay leaders, Esther and Nehemiah, and one clergyman, Ezra, confront different aspects of the same problem.

The problem: The Persian Empire was implementing a program to exterminate the Jews, starting in Persia and extending throughout the entire empire; moreover, Jerusalem lay in ruins more than a thousand miles to the west. And three Persian Jews took on this problem.

The Persian Urban Committee

Imagine a committee meeting of these three Jewish leaders, perhaps called by Nehemiah. I'm aware that scholars differ on the chronological ages of the three, but for a moment try to imagine it.

Nehemiah might open the meeting with a short statement: "As you know, we are in deep trouble. The program against our people is nearly in place here in Persia, and meanwhile my reports show that Jerusalem is a disastrous ruin."

I can imagine Esther speaking first, saying, "As you know, there has been a royal divorce. There is a vacancy in the palace. Perhaps I could enter the 'Miss Persia' contest. If I won, I would marry the king and move into the harem. Perhaps then I could confront the king about the injustice of the law and get it superseded with a higher law."

To which Nehemiah might say, "I also have a plan. I'll go to the king, ask for letters of credit and a leave of absence, and go to Jerusalem to inaugurate the model-cities development plan I have been thinking about."

To which Ezra could say, "Great idea! Esther, you move inside the system and change the law, because if we can't get the law changed or superseded, Israel has no future at all. And Nehemiah, you take the resources of the Persian Empire back to Jerusalem, because local resources, while necessary for starting the project, won't be enough to complete the city's rebuilding. Then with my contractor friend, Zerubbabel, I can rebuild the temple and the spiritual life and faith of the city."

There you have it! A lay-clergy team of men and at least one woman working for the rebuilding of Jerusalem. We need not pretend it happened exactly this way, of course, to acknowledge the unique roles of all three Persian Jews in this urban development partnership.

Esther's Role in Urban Development

Perhaps no book in the Bible is so difficult to interpret as Esther.

From my own study of the book and—perhaps equally importantly—from my own urban social location as an interpreter, I have concluded that Esther is in the Bible to remind us of four very basic theological ideas.

1. Our faith is a historical faith by which we affirm that God entered history spiritually by influencing godly people and physically by becoming incarnate in Jesus Christ. For us Christians, all earthly historic details take on significance. *Nothing* is unimportant to God, even clandestine dinner parties and the political coups of so-called pagan governments.

2. The conflict between protagonists Haman, a descendant of Amalek, and Mordecai, a Jewish descendant of Moses, reminds us that sin is often much more than personal. This battle started as a personal vendetta between Moses and Amalek (Ex 17:8-13; Deut 25:17-19). Amalekites were descendants of Esau (1 Sam 15:2). Esau's family faced continued expansion and now threatened annihilation. Then the feud became familial or tribal in Saul's lifetime (1 Sam 15). But now this historic enmity has been written into an unjust law. It is not enough to repent of this sin. The law must be changed. Let me illustrate this.

A clergy colleague of mine spent a day in Chicago's housing court watching as the judge threw out case after case of renters of slum buildings. He always sided with the slumlords, those absentee real estate speculators, against the poor people. Finally my friend could stand it no longer. He spoke up: "Your honor, if it pleases the court, may I ask, Where is the justice in this court? I've been here all day and I've seen no justice whatsoever."

The judge quickly replied, "Reverend, this is not a court of justice. This is a court of law. If you want justice, change the law!"

I've never heard the issue more forcibly stated. We must go beyond repentance and forgiveness when confronting urban sins, simply because so many of these sins are no longer personal. They have been written into bad and unjust laws. That's why we need advocacy in legislatures and courtrooms—advocacy presented by spiritually motivated, legally competent lawyers.

3. Esther is in the Bible to help us think theologically about our vocational calling when it takes us off the theologically safe maps of everyday Christianity. The word *God* does not occur in this book. It was inconceivable to many devout Jews in ancient times that God could call God-fearing believers into a Persian palace for a divine mission, in this case to change or replace an unjust law.

Let Esther's harem represent every unclean political or commercial institution or structure where evil reigns and must be confronted. Believers are needed there. Normally we receive God's guidance by serious study of the whole Bible. We obey the commands and we follow biblical examples. But what if there are no models? At that point we do what Mordecai tells Esther (4:4): we do theological reflection. Esther opens a window from which we can look at the facts of our situation from God's perspective. Paul does the same thing in Philemon 15, reflecting on a runaway slave, seeing that in the case of Onesimus, the international refugee, God "may have a larger plan."

Our cities are full of dens of iniquity. Our culture is described as essentially post-Christian, secular and often totally antithetical to biblical values and hostile to biblical virtues. Evil is multiplying, and the poor are increasingly in double jeopardy. To borrow again the language of Hong Kong minister Raymond Fung, "The poor are not only sinners; most often they are also the sinned against."

So Esther gives us permission to reflect on our call to serve God within the matrix of a modern secular or oppressive system to confront evil and work for justice. The Qumran separatists could never understand it, and modern Puritans I know won't admit it either. How could God call Esther to be the interracial replacement spouse of a polygamous, pagan Persian king? Come to think of it, this book is off the screen for many evangelicals as well. We urban people need Esther now more than ever. Never allow it to be trivialized or spiritualized away, as it has been so often in my generation.

4. Esther teaches us how to celebrate even when we are not liberated from our places of oppression. Passover celebrates Israel's deliverance from centuries of oppression in Egypt and must be remembered soberly and carefully. But Esther's feast, Purim, by contrast, is Israel's celebration originating in the Persian oppression. It celebrates God's preservation in the place of oppression when, for one reason or another, you are unable to leave. In this case, the rabbis suggest, it should be remembered with eating, drinking and a carefree spirit.

Jews have survived in ghettos all over God's earth because of the identity and hope implicit in both of these contrasting feasts. Here is my permission for great parties in the city. Believe me when I say, "A spirituality without joyful parties won't survive in the city."

Nehemiah: The Community Organizer

Nehemiah, like Esther, was a political operative, an insider. He secured the grant, the letter of credit and leave of absence for the city's rebuilding program. Nehemiah prayed and acted. Over the years I've heard many sermons about his prayer life. That's important, of course, but so is what he did, which was community organizing and development. More than anyone in Scripture, this lay leader integrates the necessary perspectives and action needed to transform cities today. He is a favorite of every urban minister I have ever met. So if anything, I'll probably short-change this story, because most of the time I find Esther's contributions ignored and Nehemiah's exaggerated.

We watch in admiration as he does his careful survey work at night (2:12-16) and then mobilizes the entire community to rebuild the wall. He did not use his Persian line of credit to bring in a professional construction crew to build the wall for the people. He understood that for the exploited city dwellers, this wall was as much for identity as security. The community, both believers and unbelievers, worked on that wall with their own hands. He approached the people not as victims who needed him, but as people with the capacity to change their situation. That's critically important. Nehemiah understood the ecological reality that a healthy community is a crucial support system for healthy persons and families.

Nehemiah confirms my own experience of watching and doing urban ministry for nearly four decades. You don't start by planting churches. You plant ministry that "scratches where people itch" in the name of Jesus. The ministries will generate the necessary ingredients for healthy churches in the long run: first, indigenous leadership; second, local funds. People who come into urban communities from outside with timetables for church planting almost inevitably create the church in the image of the outside leaders. They usually require long-term sustaining funds as well. Nehemiah empowered the local people at the outset, both the just and the unjust. He understood that his call was public leadership for all the people, not just those who possessed his high level of spirituality.

Much more could be said, of course, but 11:1-2 introduces another feature of his urban development plan. Nehemiah realized that once the wall was completed, the city was a little like Berlin after the war but with a nice wall around it. The next question was how to rebuild individual sections of the city, a problem facing every city in North America, if not the world, today.

His solution was audacious and creative. He went to the small towns and suburbs where the people lived and asked for a human tithe, one out of every ten, to come and live in Jerusalem—the big, bad city.

The Ten Percent Solution: Tithing Godly People into Godless Places
The people agreed. They not only chose the ten percent who would relocate, but laid hands on them, ordaining them for the task. For

many years I have pled with pastors to reexamine this strategy for our day. Frankly, if pastors and congregations do not have a concrete plan to move some resourceful, Spirit-filled laity into the worst sections of the communities around their church buildings, then I maintain that they really don't believe in tithing. Furthermore, they inevitably will produce a commuting congregation and a clubhouse church building quite alienated from their nearest neighbors.

I also argue that a tithe or ten percent solution is enough. If you relocate more than that, you'll intimidate the neighbors and probably gentrify the neighborhood, thereby displacing the very people you've come to help.

When Esther and Nehemiah had done their work, Ezra could follow his call as clergy to oversee the building of the temple and the process of rebuilding the faith of the people.

The "three Persians" remind us it takes a strong long-term partnership to rebuild urban communities, especially those ravaged by war and Sanballat-like political machines that exist in codependent fashion to exploit the vulnerable masses who fall through the cracks of success cultures.

This partnership also reminds us that both men and women are needed on the team. Many of us remember the missionary story of five men martyred while trying to reach the Auca Indians in Ecuador in the 1950s. Then the women and children moved into the village to live with those who had slain their men. The village came to Jesus! I've noticed over many years a similar urban phenomenon. Some American city communities are so violent that only women will be safe and effective as evangelists, pastors and church planters. Their vulnerability is their power in many emasculated, gang-ridden neighborhoods. I've also seen this pattern in repeated visits to places like Beirut and Belfast over the years. The men are dead or not trusted. The women are building God's church.

There are other important lessons from this story. It reminds us that outsiders can play a role in local community development, because they can access much-needed resources. Grace is an outside gift today as well. We also note that it took more than a half-century to rebuild Jerusalem and reestablish the temple—and that was with prayers, great leaders, resources and the leading of God. It will take more than those marvelous Jesus marches and regular prayer walks and a few wonderful congregations to do the job of rebuilding cities. The sin in our cities is real and entrenched. It will take time.

I think of the "three Persians," reaching back to serve God in Israel, as half of Israel's international ministry in the Old Testament. The other half is God's commissioning of Jonah to carry the gospel to Nineveh (the northern capital city of modern Iraq today). The greatest recorded revival in the Hebrew Bible, before Pentecost, is off the map of Israel, over in the Assyrian capital city.

14
MODELS FROM THE
MIGRANT STREAMS
THE INTERTESTAMENTAL ERA

Now these Jews are already gotten into all cities;
and it is hard to find a place in the habitable earth
that hath not admitted this tribe of men,
and is not possessed by them.
Josephus Antiquities 14.7.2

THE INTERTESTAMENTAL ERA, THAT four-hundred-year period between Malachi and Matthew, is anything but a silent time. Israel was
dispersed into the cities of the Assyrian, Babylonian, Persian, Egyptian, Greek and Roman worlds.

When the Jews no longer lived in Palestine within reach of their
temple and priesthood and were no longer surrounded by the
Hebrew language, amazing differences began to appear in Judaism.
You can see what was happening even as you read Daniel and the
last books written in the Old Testament. For one thing, Aramaisms,
which reflected the language people spoke in some places, began to
creep into the Hebrew Bible.

Many scholars have documented this, but two of them made the
earliest impact on me. One was G. F. Moore, who wrote in his two
volumes on first-century Judaism and the religious context of the
New Testament era that the flower garden of first-century Judaism
was far more variegated than we had supposed.[1]

The other was New Testament scholar Richard Longenecker, who had a major influence on my thought, especially in regard to the intertestamental period.

Two institutions "invented" in the Jewish urban diaspora had special consequences for the rapid spread of Christianity: the synagogue and the Septuagint (a Greek version of the Old Testament Scriptures). I agree with Michael Green's statement in *Evangelism in the Early Church* that you can't possibly explain the rapid spread of Christianity in the early Christian era without reference to the roles played by these Jewish contributions borrowed for the Christian mission.[2]

I remember reading, in the 1960s, Jewish scholar Louis Finkelstein's discussion on the sociological implications of the rise of the Pharisees[3] and saying to myself, *These people are kin to the Plymouth Brethren of our own era.* Of course the analogy does break down, but the Pharisees were a lay movement as are the Brethren, centered upon the Bible with no clergy or ecclesiastical rituals, organized around portable theological institutions called "synagogues." A core group of Jewish men could organize one. In time they came to rival the professional clergy and their temple "priest-craft" tradition, which after all looked a bit like the established churches of Europe over time.

The Brethren movement I'm talking about began in the United Kingdom after 1830, and many leaders were laypeople working in the British military and foreign service. The British colonized fifty-two nations. I've visited most of them, and the pattern is familiar. Wherever the British went you will find a large Anglican church prominently located near town center. Nearby, perhaps across the square, will be the Methodist church, and on a nearby side street you will find the Brethren chapel. The Brethren went everywhere, and some did become a little legalistic and biblicistic at times, but they've stayed in those cities to this day.

The synagogues of the Pharisees came back to Israel and then spread wherever Jews were dispersed. In time some of them became churches (see Jas 2:1).

The Septuagint was translated over many years in Alexandria, Egypt, a long-time center of Jewish and Greek scholarship, which was reported to have the greatest library of the ancient world. At one time, Jews in Alexandria may have accounted for as much as one-third of the total population.[4]

The language that tied the Greek-Roman empire together was Koine, or common Greek, not the rich classical Greek of Athens. It was more like Swahili in East Africa, a trade language.

Can you imagine the arduous task of translating the complexity of the Old Testament text into common street Greek? Isaiah alone has more vocabulary than all twenty-seven books of the New Testament combined. Imagine how painful it must have been for the scholars and the elderly. They may have done this to save their children, but Pentecost fanned their flame, and they helped save the world.

Eventually this Greek Bible came back to Palestine and was quoted by Peter at Pentecost, when he cited the text from Joel (Acts 2). This Bible was used by Jewish Christians all over the Roman world and later by Greek and Roman Christians as well.

Shortly after exploring this history, I read the magnificent two-volume study by the late Methodist historian Frederick Norwood called *Strangers and Exiles: A History of Religious Refugees*.[5] Norwood spent his life expanding the research done under Roland Bainton at Yale. His two volumes trace refugee theology from Abraham (2000 B.C.) to the mid 1960s.

One can read church history by studying its center—canons, creeds and church leaders (three *c*'s)[6]—or by studying it from the frontiers of faith where Christianity crossed cultures and was impacted by them in return. Kenneth Scott Latourette is an example of one who studied from the frontier or mission starting point.[7] Norwood follows Latourette in taking the single theme of how God has used religious refugees to change the world. We should stop seeing refugees merely as victims, for they have been God's agents to spread the gospel for four thousand years.

Faith on the Frontiers

Perhaps now you can see how these interdisciplinary studies began to impact my view of God's church in God's world. As I've already mentioned, the twentieth century has produced the greatest global migration in the history of the world. The Southern hemisphere is coming North; East is coming West and everyone is coming to the cities. History does not repeat, but patterns reappear from time to time.

The United States, the largest Jewish nation, the largest Irish and Scandinavian nation, is now the second-largest African nation (after Nigeria) and probably the third-largest Spanish-speaking nation. The whole British Empire now lives in London. Bradford near Leeds was rapidly Asianizing a decade ago. Paris is 14 percent African; Turks live in Germany, Indonesians in Amsterdam, a million Japanese in São Paulo, Brazil; and perhaps as many as 90 million Chinese live outside mainland China.

Does all this movement surprise the Lord of history? I think not. These migrating peoples are going to school in every major city in the world. The Chinese, like the diaspora Jews two thousand years ago, are learning the world's languages and networking back to the mainland of China.

Over the years I've visited and preached in many bilingual or multilingual urban churches. I pastored one. The lessons the Korean Presbyterians and Pentecostals are learning today in Flushing, New York (where there are already more than 600 Korean churches), are the same lessons the Jews learned in the diaspora. The children are becoming bilingual. Texts are being translated.

There is a marvelous line in Paul's letter to the Galatians (4:4): "But when the time had fully come, God sent his Son." The "time" referred to was not chronological time. Rather, the Greek word refers to "opportune time."

God's divine choreography permitted successive civilizations—Babylonian, Greek, Roman and Jewish—to help set the stage. One could travel from Britain to India in Paul's day and for the most part use the Greek trade language with one Roman passport.

The intertestamental era of biblical studies provides a hermeneutical window for me to see how God's evangelization plan may be operating. My urban ministry lens has greatly expanded. I resonate with Paul in his Philemon reflection on the slave Onesimus's international migration: "Perhaps this is why . . ." These texts provide permission to "read" the world.

For the first time ever, by about the year 2000 over 50 percent of the people on the planet will live in cities. Cities have replaced the nations. Yesterday, cities were in the nations; today all the nations are in our cities. The fuse is nearly lit for an Asian twenty-first-century Pentecost. Could it be? I think so. I see a familiar pattern here, and it has changed the way I see my city.

Impact Everywhere

Urban ministry has emerged in my lifetime with five specializations on each continent:

1. Rescue ministry to the "at-risk" populations, including relief and evangelization of the world's most vulnerable peoples

2. Church-based community organizing and development

3. Ethnic ministries—both multilingual and multicultural

4. Lay empowerment for vocational ministries within the city's public square

5. Congregational adaptations of traditional ministry functions to the urban context

Many years ago a famous Chicago pastor named Harry Ironside wrote a little book titled *The 400 Silent Years*.[8] From where we sit today, these intertestamental years were anything but silent. You see, it's often a matter of vantage point. If we measure church growth in Tokyo, the numbers may disappoint us. But if we could map the impact that the Korean, Chinese, Filipino, Brazilian-Japanese and Indonesian congregations in Tokyo have back in their home countries, I believe we would read the data very differently.

The oldest churches in Christendom, the Antiochene, Coptic, Assyrian and Greek churches, are the newest churches in my Chicago neighborhood. Surely this represents some loss for those measuring the church in Cairo. But is it really loss, or is God molding a new generation of Arab-speaking evangelists for the Arab-Americans who will outnumber Jews here by A.D. 2000?

We come now to the threshold of the New Testament in what I have called "the search for a theology as big as the city." Perhaps you are ready to agree with me that both the city and a biblically oriented theology are bigger than we ever dreamed.

15
SKELETONS IN THE CLOSET
THE OTHER WOMEN IN THE FAMILY OF JESUS

A record of the genealogy of Jesus Christ
the son of David, the son of Abraham . . .
The Good News According to Matthew 1:1

I'VE OFTEN WONDERED WHY the "good news according to Matthew" begins by taking us on a cemetery tour. Why is that list of dead people good news?

The earliest Christians certainly did not emphasize the birth or family lineage of Jesus. They hardly mentioned it. As far as we can tell, Peter and Paul never told anyone to go down to Bethlehem and interview shepherds, wise men or innkeepers.

In fact, the earliest Christians were completely caught up in knowing that the earthly Jesus died on the cross, was resurrected, ascended to heaven, and now is the triumphant Lord of Glory whose "name," they finally realized, was none other than the very "I AM" of Exodus 6:2-8 (see Acts 3:6, 16). The early church was so excited to learn who this Jesus was that they only had time to rejoice in his power, glory and majesty. This is what they sang hymns about (Phil 2:5-11, for example, was probably an early hymn).

In the same first-century Asian communities, there was a growing emphasis on an Eastern mysticism that grew into Gnosticism; it could be considered the ancient equivalent of the New Age movement. Gnostics loved the idea that Jesus was a heavenly spirit. Like Plato, they never could accept the idea that a good God could be incarnate physically with real flesh and blood.

Gnosticism was very strong in Asia Minor near Laodicea and Colossae. You can hear some echoes in Paul and John as they stress: "For in Christ all the fullness of the Deity lives in *bodily* form" [italics mine] (Col 2:9), or "That . . . which we have heard, which we have seen with our eyes, which we have looked at and our hands have touched—this we proclaim concerning the Word of life" (1 Jn 1:1).

The word *gnostic* comes from the Greek word for knowledge. Gnostics claimed to have special secret knowledge. In their world of good and evil, material bodies are evil, and our spirits are trapped in our bodies. A special wisdom was necessary to escape into cosmic safety zones of light. They claimed to have the secrets to this speculative mystical salvation.

Paul, of course, argued against this repeatedly in his letters to the Colossians (2:8-23) and to Timothy and Titus, for the threat to the historic Christian faith was very real.

The Recovery of the Birth Stories

At some point rather late in the New Testament era, both Matthew and Luke realized there was a problem. Like Professor Raymond Brown, I think the infancy narratives of Matthew and Luke came as a result of the "wake-up call" Gnosticism presented to the church.[1]

Like the overtures of an opera or operetta, the infancy narratives of Matthew and Luke may have been the last parts of their Gospels to be written, because in these opening chapters most of the themes of those Gospels appear briefly.

Both birth accounts link Jesus the man to a political and geographic space. Matthew shows how Jesus recapitulated the history of Israel, making the trip to Egypt and later spending a day in the wilderness for each year Moses spent there.

Luke, the only non-Jewish writer in the New Testament, traces Jesus' genealogy back farther, beyond Abraham, all the way back to Adam. For Luke, Jesus is not merely an ethnic savior. He is God's message to the Roman Empire.

In Matthew's genealogy we notice that Israel's history is summarized in three epochs, each with fourteen names. We also notice by comparing the genealogies in Exodus 6 and 1 Chronicles that Matthew has deliberately selected some names and excluded others. The Hebrew phrase "son of" is so elastic that it can be stretched to say "Jesus is the son of David, the son of Abraham." There are a thousand years between some names. Obviously there are gaps of various lengths in the lists.

All this makes it even more special that in the opening paragraph of our cemetery tour, Matthew takes us to four very ancient graves in the oldest sections of Israel's burial ground.

A record of the genealogy of Jesus Christ the son of David, the son of Abraham:

Abraham was the father of Isaac,

    Isaac the father of Jacob,

    Jacob the father of Judah and his brothers,

    Judah the father of Perez and Zerah, whose mother was Tamar,

    Perez the father of Hezron,

    Hezron the father of Ram,

    Ram the father of Amminadab,

    Amminadab the father of Nahshon,

    Nahshon the father of Salmon,

    Salmon the father of Boaz, whose mother was Rahab,

    Boaz the father of Obed, whose mother was Ruth,

    Obed the father of Jesse,

    and Jesse the father of King David.

David was the father of Solomon, whose mother had been Uriah's wife.[2] (Mt 1:1-6)

Later in this chapter Matthew goes on to tell the story of how the virgin Mary became Jesus' mother—a rather scandalous story. Rahab, Ruth and Bathsheba, all included in the genealogy, are what I call the "grandmothers of Christmas past." Both Matthew and I insist they are part of the Christmas story.

Movie makers would give these stories an R rating. Let's review them briefly.[3]

Tamar

In the midst of the Joseph story (Gen 37—50), the author flashes back to reveal another side of the miraculous providence in the Joseph story. Tamar married the first two sons of Judah and outlived them both. She was denied marriage to the third son, thus breaking local Levirite marriage laws, and she returned to her village. (As the father of three sons, I can understand Judah's reluctance to have her "devour" all three of his boys!)

Sometime later, she decided to intervene in Judah's life (Gen 38). She dressed as a prostitute and had a sexual affair with him. He could not pay her, so he left his "credit card" (his signature ring with its cord and his walking stick). Later Judah heard Tamar was pregnant and ordered she be executed. When asked who the father was, she produced the "credit card," and Judah's hypocrisy was exposed. Tamar had twins, one of whom is an ancestor of Jesus.

Rahab

Rahab ran a hotel in Jericho (Josh 2:1-24; 6:22-25). We gain insight into what type of hotel this was from James 2:25, which uses the word *pornē* to describe Rahab. It was an urban place where lights are low and no one asks your name, making it an obvious place for spies to go and hide.

When the Jericho Gestapo entered Rahab's hotel, she hid the spies, then lied to the police and put them on a false trail. Then she told the spies of her faith in the God of Israel. She'd heard of the exodus and the miracles. It was obviously her faith that saved her. Nothing else could, right?

Ruth of Moab

While Ruth is never called a sinner, her culture and family tree come from Sodom (see chapter five of this book for further discussion). Despite her background, she became the great-grandmother of King David and therefore an ancestor of Jesus.

Bathsheba the Wife of Uriah

With Israel's middle management off at war in Rehobeth (modern Amman, Jordan), David was clearly bored. It had been some time since he had written a song, played a harp or killed a giant. So he got sexually involved with a beautiful neighbor (2 Sam 11:1—12:25). This neighbor's husband happened to be David's best soldier, Uriah. Sometime later she sent him word back at the palace: "I'm pregnant."

David initiated a plan to "take care of" this problem. First he wrote to General Joab and ordered him to send Uriah home for some R&R. If Uriah slept with his wife, perhaps he (and others) wouldn't suspect that the child wasn't his. But it didn't work. Uriah, a noble soldier, refused to indulge his own pleasure while his brothers were at war.

Plan two involved a state dinner with lots of drinking. Perhaps under the influence Uriah would go home. But again it didn't work.

In desperation, David moved to plan three. As commander-in-chief, he directed his field general to fight all the way up to the wall with Uriah on the point, then retreat quickly. This was a risky, even foolish maneuver, because all the enemy needed to do was drop rocks on the heads of those close to the wall, and they were as good as dead. It worked. Uriah never knew. David married the publicly grieving widow in a state marriage. His "ratings" doubtless went up in the polls. But a prophet exposed David's sin. The baby died soon after birth. Their second child was Solomon.

Explanations

Now the question remains: Why are these four women in the opening paragraph of our New Testament in Matthew's "Good News"?

Jerome in the fourth century suggested that all four women were sinners and that Jesus came into the world to save women like them. The problem with this interpretation is that all the men in the text were also terrible sinners. There must be a further word.

Luther was the first one who noticed (in print) that all four women were *foreigners*.[4] Two were Canaanites (Tamar and Rahab); Ruth was Moabite; Bathsheba was presumably Hittite. These texts are about missions! Stephen Neill, long-time missionary in India and mission historian, wrote a marvelously helpful book called *The Interpretation of the New Testament 1861-1961,* in which he amplifies Luther's view that these women represent Matthew's foreign mission concern. Neill suggests there is an international parenthesis around Matthew's Gospel.[5] Chapter 28 tells the disciples to go into all the world, preach the gospel and disciple all peoples. But Matthew 1 helps us remember who "the world's peoples" were at that time. They included Canaanites, Moabites, Hittites and Jews, among others.

In a tongue-in-cheek fashion, Raymond Brown of Union Seminary offers yet another idea.[6] Perhaps Matthew provides pastoral care for Mary by bringing together all the scandalous birth stories as a kind of historical support group, because Mary was having a very difficult time explaining where her own baby came from. So "Mary, you are not alone" is the message.

Professor Eduard Schweizer of Zurich offers a different idea.[7] It seems that after the ascension of Jesus, the disciples split up, and Matthew ended up pastoring a non-Jewish church in Syria, off the map of Israel. Some people might have wondered whether people outside of Israel could really be saved.

Matthew's answer was "Yes!" Not only the ecclesial fruit, but the historic roots of Israel go outside the ethnic boundaries. Jesus was (on his human side) the product of an international family tree. As nearly as I have been able to discern from my study of these genealogies, these four women were ancestors of both Mary and Joseph. The families of Mary and Joseph seem to split after David, making the women biologically his maternal grandparents on his earthly side.

I would also note another common element: that all four of these women took initiative, acted remarkably with courage and received divine approval.

Matthew is making an important theological statement about Jesus. On his divine side, Jesus was the virgin-born son of God. Let there be no doubt about that. The creeds point to the virgin birth for good reason; it is inspiring truth. Christianity is no bootstrap, self-help religion. Barth was right; the virgin birth reminds us that salvation is God reaching down to us. Grace is an outside gift.

But on the human side, Matthew reminds us (against certain mystics both then and now) that Jesus was also very human indeed. He choreographed into his own earthly body all the most theologically sinful bloodlines in the Middle East. In a very real sense, this opening paragraph smashes racism. Jesus was the mixed-racial Savior of the world.

Now here's how Christmas and Easter connect for Matthew. Jesus not only got his blood from the world, he also shed that blood on the cross for the world. The blood of Canaanites from the cursed race of Canaan (Gen 9), the Sodomites (Gen 18; Ruth), Hittites and Jews was shed on the cross and accepted by a priesthood as the offering atonement for my sin. But it was not only my sin that was atoned for. All the sins of every racial group in my city are included.

For years I pastored urban people of mixed-racial families whose earthly identity was never clear to them. Many fell through the social cracks of our race-conscious society. What a joy it was to tell them about Matthew's "Grandmothers of Christmas." We are all children of Adam and therefore sinful, but we are one in Christ. There is no theological distinction (Gal 3:28) between race (Jew or Gentile), class (slave or free) or sex (male or female).

Despite this gospel message, America and its cities are resegregating around issues of race, class and sex again today. Some people remind me of the ancient mystics when they say, "Can't we just rise above all this and forget these 'issues' once and for all? Can't we just concentrate on spiritual things and avoid all the controversy?"

I think Matthew would say no. On the contrary, he would drag us back into our histories. Our roots expose our mutually sinful ancestors and rub our noses in the stuff of our own sinfulness. Therefore, any sense of human superiority is crushed at the foot of Christ's cross.

At first glimpse this may sound like bad news, but it's really very good news indeed. Thank God for Matthew's cemetery.

16
JESUS & THE CITY
THE SEARCH FOR AN URBAN JESUS

Jesus went through all the towns and villages,
teaching in their synagogues, preaching the good news
of the kingdom and healing every disease and sickness.
Matthew 9:35

THE JESUS OF MY CHILDHOOD was hardly "gentle Jesus, meek and mild." As I was from an athletic family, my Jesus probably bordered on the *macho* side. But he certainly lacked both color and ethnicity.

The Bible-institute Jesus of the 1950s tended to be locked in a time warp. He was virgin-born, significant at the cross, but safe in heaven now and getting ready for the big activities of the future—the rapture, the millennium and Judgment Day.

In this view, Jesus was spiritually, but not ethnically, Jewish—clearly not a model for life or spirituality of the city. Clearly in the dispensationalist understanding of the "lingering Cold War" era and after the 1948 founding of Israel, the Bible study emphasis was in the Epistles and not the Gospels. Coming as I did from a Lutheran pietist background, I never felt comfortable with the Jesus of dispensationalist evangelicalism, but I didn't know why.

My own search for the Jesus of the Gospels who could also be both personal Savior and Lord of my city began when I was a twenty-one-year-old, temporarily out of work but with a burning passion to find the truth about Jesus for myself. I wanted to learn as much as I could about the time, place and culture where Jesus lived and ministered, and then to read the Gospels with a fresh understanding of Jesus' message and model for ministry.

The Search for Truth

It was in my quest to learn about Jesus that I came to a revolutionary realization: my understanding and love for Jesus could withstand and even be enhanced by studying more than one point of view.

I date this "intellectual conversion" to late June 1959, at about 2 p.m., in the city library of Fairbanks, Alaska. My dad was reading nearby. I had graduated from Moody Bible Institute a few weeks earlier, where I had heard that the Dead Sea Scrolls (discovered twelve years before) would shed great light on Jesus but not all of it would be complimentary.

My dad and I had gone to Alaska to work in construction. I was planning to begin college and ministry that fall in Seattle and needed extra funds. Unfortunately, there was no work to be found in Alaska. Everyone was on strike, and rains had put out the forest fires. I had four weeks to search for work, but all I found were three libraries— one at a nearby military base, one at the University of Alaska (an hour's walk from Fairbanks) and the city library. I didn't earn any money, but I read a ton of books.

Amazingly, I found several new titles on the Dead Sea Scrolls. Edmund Wilson's popular paperback presented Jesus as a faint copy of the Qumran "teacher of righteousness," with whom Jesus had studied before going into public ministry.[1] John Allegro had a similar theory, which was even more radical.[2]

I then read *The Dead Sea Scrolls,* written by a classic liberal scholar, Millar Burrows.[3] Rather than detract from my conception of Jesus, this volume helped me to appreciate how the scrolls could illuminate Jesus' social milieu. Encouraged by what I had read in the first book, I delved into Burrows's second volume, *More Light on the Dead Sea Scrolls*. Even after thirty-seven years, I can still visualize the page that sparked my "conversion." It was chapter four, the first page, second paragraph, second sentence:

> Were I to debate a professor from the Fordham University [by which he meant conservative Catholic], or the Moody Bible Institute [by which he meant conservative Protestant], I feel I should have no ammunition to use against them.[4]

I said "Hallelujah!" out loud, startling both my dad and Mrs. Hoke, the librarian, who were the only others there.

In my last semester at Moody I had asked the professor of one of my least favorite classes if he could recommend a good liberal book on the scrolls. I sensed I was getting the "party line" in his course, and I was increasingly suspicious. Not only did he not mention such a book, but he said that to do so would dishonor the walls of our sacred school. Yet here I found a theological "liberal" (Burrows) who was willing to acknowledge that there were other points of view. His acknowledgment of his bias was the prod I needed. I can learn from anybody if I ask God to overcome my own bias.

Locating Jesus in Place and Time

My study of the Dead Sea Scrolls whetted my appetite for learning about what life was like when Jesus was alive. Fortunately, rather early in my Gospel studies I came across Harvard New Testament professor Henry Cadbury's book *The Perils of Modernizing Jesus*.[5] He recognized that there was a fine line between the historical recovery of the text and the bias of the researcher looking for answers.

My dear sister Marilyn helped me to recover the ethnicity of Jesus by giving me the two-volume set of Alfred Edersheim's *The Life and Times of Jesus the Messiah* as a Christmas present in 1959.[6] (You could probably fit all the younger sisters who buy their minister brothers theology books into one phone booth. In those preseminary days, I preached two or more times each week, and she knew

I needed all the help I could get.)

Not only the person of Jesus but the context of Jesus' life in Galilee required a radical revision from my childhood Bible story pictures. First-century Palestine was a far more international and politicized environment than the Sunday-school literature had communicated.

Four miles north of Nazareth lay the government's great regional capital city of Sepphoris, rebuilt mostly during Jesus' Nazareth years by Herod Antipas, one of Herod's three sons, who ruled the region for Rome. The Galilee Jesus knew was busy with government policies and personnel, economically diverse classes and an entertainment industry that included actors for major productions in a huge theater!

Matthew and Mark tell us Jesus went about all the cities and villages of Galilee (Mt 9:35—11:1; Mk 6:6, 56). That would be an area twenty-five to thirty miles across in both east-west and north-south directions. Josephus tells us there were more than two hundred cities and villages in Galilee.

We are fortunate now to have the published research of Richard A. Batey, *Jesus and the Forgotten City: New Light on Sepphoris and the Urban World of Jesus.*[7] Paul L. Maier, in the foreword, reminds us that this research pushes us beyond the pastoral rural-redeemer image to the city-savior image of Jesus as well. It's a much more balanced portrait. I agree with Maier's assessment. This research is helpful for biblical studies today, but it's probably not the last word on the subject either.

> The city not only edged dramatically into Jesus' life and ministry but subsequently became central to the future expansion of Christianity. It was from such metropolises as Antioch, Alexandria, Ephesus, Athens, Corinth and Rome that the gospel was carried into the countryside, where the rural sorts—the *pagani* (hence the term *pagan*)—were the last to convert. This Christianity which began in hamlets like Bethlehem and Nazareth in the person of Jesus finally came full circle through the mediation of urban culture.[8]

Jesus in the Decapolis

The urban milieu of Jesus goes far beyond Galilee. In 1984 I finally visited Jerash in North Jordan, high in the Gilead hills, with its elegant forum and magnificent theater still in use. This was one of the ten cities called Decapolis where Jesus ministered and to which apostles (the former disciples) carried the gospel after Pentecost. The Decapolis represented the political and cultural hegemony of the Greeks going back three hundred years before Christ. British scholar N. G. L. Hammond, in his study of Alexander the Great, suggests that these cities represented nearly total Macedonian control of the region, the area in Transjordan from Moab to Damascus.[9]

Jesus' message spread through these areas, according to Matthew 4:25 and Mark 5:20, 31. In his 1982 scholarly book *Jerash and the Decapolis,* Iain Browning describes the highly organized society:

At the center of it was the concept of the *polis* with its organized, polished, economic, administrative, as well as philosophical and social implications. It was a fundamental concept which was to spread to all lands and peoples who were touched by Greek culture, even to Rome itself (Pliny in the first century uses the word *civitas* to describe such communities). The resulting Hellenism, i.e., Greek language, produced a cosmopolitan fraternity which vaulted the narrow bounds of mere race or nationality.[10]

Rome merely reorganized and centralized these Greek social and cultural realities, and the milieu spread throughout Palestine and in the whole Near East. There was no place to hide from these influences. The populations then were as large or larger than those in the same areas today, according to various scholars. There was far more to Galilee than shepherds, fields and olive groves.

Why the disciples as apostles could transition so easily from Palestine to the cities of Rome's empire can now be understood. The disciples were not so parochial or so "pale" as we might have supposed. They were prepared to follow Jesus in an urbanized world, because that is where and how they were discipled. They were multienvironmental people, and, as G. F. Moore reminds us, even Judaism in the Palestinian or Diaspora variety was far more pluralistic than we can probably imagine today.[11]

An Urban Message

The late professor Robert Guelich, a faculty colleague, friend and marvelous communicator on the gospel genre, was fond of asking students whether the Gospel word pictures of Jesus were photographs, portraits or abstract paintings. He argued that they were portrait images, because—unlike photographs—the writers' biases project into the portrait, but—unlike abstract paintings—the writers' biases don't overwhelm the person, work and context. The portraits we see of Jesus in the Gospels show him teaching in urban contexts, addressing urban themes.

George Eldon Ladd helped me early on to see the significance and powerful presence of the kingdom in the Gospels and as the centerpiece of Jesus' teaching.[12] The reign of God has begun, but it is also yet to come in its fullness. This means the salvation message goes beyond the merely personal to address our whole society, its structures and its systems. The kingdom includes the work of the church, but the reign of God is a larger concept and the work of the church is accountable to the kingdom.

In fact, as I began to explore the kingdom in the Gospels and the rest of the New Testament, it became clear that the nature and work of the church includes two basic ideas: first, to be a sign of the kingdom, and, second, to be an agent for it in the world.

Matthew's portrait of Jesus' concern for justice and righteousness and his passion for going beyond belief to discipleship and teaching cannot be contained by rural modes and metaphors.

Mark choreographs Jesus' ministry in Galilee around the lake, touching numerous urban environments, including the east-side Necropolis, city of the dead (Mk 4—5). The two storms portrayed (one environmental and the other personal) and the two dying women in the city are urban portraits.

The very architecture of Luke-Acts, which moves from Galilee to Jerusalem and then from Jerusalem to Rome, displays an urban focus. Luke's emphasis on ethnicity (especially Samaritans) as well as all the social themes of riches, poverty, justice and women make up the urban agenda. The book climaxes with a command to remain in the city until Pentecost (Lk 24).

In John the seven miracle stories as well as the contrasting portraits of persons command our attention. Contrast, for example, Nicodemus in John 3 with the Samaritan woman in John 4. Nicodemus—upper-class, kosher and elite—was met indoors in the night and teased with the image of wind. The woman of Samaria—a social outcast—was met outdoors in midday and teased with the image of water. Nicodemus reappears in chapter 7 at the illegal Sanhedrin meeting and again in chapter 19 where he publicly identifies with the dead body of Jesus. The cross convinced him, but as with many scholars and intellectuals, his conversion was a long process of enormous mental and ideological significance.

The Samaritan woman, by contrast, was offered the option of forgiveness, and for that she delivered her town to Jesus. Moreover, John notes how Jesus stayed with her and accepted her "significant others," a pathological network of family and community (4:39-41). This had incredible significance for the ethnic urban evangelism I was engaged in for so many years. Interspersed among the diverse miracle stories made powerful by the Jewish background are the stories of people coming to faith in Jesus in many different ways. John's point of view is clearly broader than sheep and shepherd metaphors.

Sacred Places

Jesus made a comment to Nathaniel about angels ascending and descending (Jn 1:50-51), an oblique reference to Jacob's story in Genesis 28. Raymond Brown's exegesis of this passage helped me recover the doctrine of holy space in the New Testament.[13] Brown reports that the place where heaven's host touched earth is holy. It is called Bethel, a house of God, where Jews built altars. It's Mecca or Haj pilgrimage theology in Islam.

By transferring the Hebrew concept of sacred place onto himself, Jesus broadens the idea rather than removes it. Jesus does not cut us free of the "sacred space" concept; he transforms it. So any place Jesus goes is "Bethel." Every ghetto I ever visited had at least one follower of Jesus living there. It's not a *bad* neighborhood. Take off your shoes—it's holy ground. Concepts like this change your view of neighborhoods and communities. Evangelism includes both the spiritual transformation of persons and the social transformation of places.

W. D. Davies's book *The Gospel and the Land* helped me see that the continuities between Old and New Testaments on land concepts go far beyond a few verses.[14] I'd assumed for years that the New Testament gospel was universal in the sense that, unlike Israel, we were cut free from land or place theology to embrace person theology. We can follow Jesus personally. The gospel transcends places, families and communities.

But in both testaments people's identities are hyphenated to places (Saul of Tarsus) and families (Simon, son of Jonah). Shedd's study of Paul, *Man in Community,* was one of the texts I used over thirty years ago that convinced me that the Old Testament themes of corporate solidarity and personality carry over to the heart of Pauline theology and are rooted in Jesus' teaching also.[15] Again, the significance of this for my own theology and theory of ministry is profound.

You see, if I have rightly understood the Hebraic and contextual rootedness of Jesus, the Gospels, Paul and the Epistles, then pastors have a dual role—as shepherds of God's flock, to be sure, but also as chaplains to communities, including other pastors as well. I cannot just care about my church. At least one of my six basic ministry functions will be networking and evangelizing in my community—perhaps off the program map of my local church.

Jesus as Model for Urban Ministry

Jesus not only brought us the profound message of salvation through his life and his work on the cross; he also modeled what kingdom-building ministry and evangelism should look like. As a city person I have to think about Jesus in the context of power issues, because the city is a political matrix of institutionalized power where the gospel must win back lost peoples and lost places.

Years ago, John Howard Yoder helped me see that Jesus' message of salvation and liberation was deeply rooted in the Levitical idea of Jubilee.[16] Jesus presupposed that we don't *have* power; we *are* power. The gospel unleashes in us processes that can't be stopped, short of social transformation.

Similarly, in his book *Conversion,* Arthur Darbey Nock, a specialist at Harvard a generation ago on the history of religion, argues that Christianity took root because of the power of its ideas, not because of its public, economic or political favor.[17]

This provides a lens to help us analyze the evangelization dynamics of our times. In contrast to the early spread of Christianity, for the last two hundred years Christianity has gone from West to East on the wings of political, economic and military power. Far too often Christians have married evangelism to power and wrapped it in the trappings of triumphalist strategy and technology.

As we approach the year 2000, Nock prompts me to reassess our strategies. For me, the Jesus gospel is a "bottom up" and intimately transforming relationship. The bigger the city and the more urbanized we get, the more intentionally personal and local our witness must become. For years I've been increasingly uncomfortable with mass-evangelism strategies that are technically, financially or millennially driven. We can see many results today, almost instantly. But what of the bigger picture?

Curiously, Islam is perilously close to being financially driven by oil economics and politics. The numerical gains in the cities are rather stunning within three major streams of Islam: Arab, Asian and African. The number of mosques has doubled in Chicago in less than a decade. Saudi-funded cultural centers are certainly part of the reason.

Teresa of Calcutta has another approach. She sees Jesus in the face of the poor and dying, so to care for them is to worship Jesus (Mt 25 is her classic text). It takes seven years to become her disciple. The ministry of the Sisters of Charity is so nontechnically driven, it's off the normal modern charts. These women serve in more than a hundred cities around the world. They eschew power, and yet they possess it—even radiate it worldwide. This is kingdom power, Holy Spirit power. With it we color outside the world's lines, assaulting and transforming Satan's urban strongholds. It is the unique and profound combination of Jesus as *message* and Jesus as *model*.

The Power of Good News

Back in 1971, Scottish preacher and theology professor Murdough McDonald of Glasgow helped me understand how the gospel functions as legitimate power in society. He did so with his own personal story.

McDonald was a paratrooper in World War II. He bailed out of an airplane behind German lines, was taken prisoner with his fellow Scottish chaplain and was put in a concentration camp for many months. McDonald was put with the Americans to be a kind of chaplain to the American prisoners, while his friend was put with the British at the other end of the large camp. For some reason, the German guards would not allow the British prisoners and American prisoners to fraternize even through the high fence in the middle of the camp. But once a day they allowed the two chaplains to come and speak together—briefly, but only in the presence of guards.

Unknown to the guards, the Americans possessed a little home-made wireless radio, and they were getting news from the outside world. Murdough McDonald reported the situation: "Every day I tried to take a headline to give it to my friend through the fence. Unfortunately, the German guards spoke French and English, but we finally realized they didn't speak Gaelic. Every day I would come with a radio headline in Gaelic and give it to my friend through the fence." This went on for many months.

One day the news came over the radio that the German high command had surrendered and the war was over. No guards knew of this because all of the communication had broken down in Germany. McDonald said, "I took that news to the fence that day and I gave it to my friend, and that day I stood at the fence while my friend went into the British barracks. I waited for what I knew would happen. There was a thunderous roar of celebration from the British barracks. And the most amazing thing happened. For three days prisoners of war walked around the camp singing and shouting. We were gloriously happy! We didn't complain about the food, we waved at the dogs and the guards; no guard knew what was happening. Nobody could explain it. Every prisoner of war was rejoicing and celebrating!

"On the morning of the fourth day, we prisoners woke up and realized it was different. No guards. Apparently in the night they heard the news and slipped out into the forest; they left the gates closed but unlocked. . . . On the morning of the fourth day we walked out of the prison as freed men."

But then McDonald said something I will never forget: "We were set free four days before by *news* that the war was over."

The gospel of Jesus Christ is not advice; it's news. A fundamental difference between Ann Landers and Jesus Christ is that Ann offers advice and Jesus offers news. The gospel of Jesus changes everything inside our own prisons, be they personal, family, community or national. The gospel is never advice, and it's never a program. It's news! But when we who have power and resources link up with people in prisons who hear and believe the gospel, doors open and the Spirit empowers real and total change. It takes time, of course, and it takes city ministry partnerships that can combine the good news with good advice resources. It's bringing them together that is required, to best capture the significance of Jesus in the Gospels and the Jesus of my city nearly two thousand years later.

We patronize the poor when we give them advice. But Jesus is news, not advice. To evangelize the urban poor, or the affluent poor for that matter, is to liberate them with the news that the ultimate victory is won; the war is over! With this message of hope we can begin the liberation program.

17
THE CHURCH AT
THE CITY CENTER
FROM PENTECOST TO ANTIOCH
(ACTS 1—12)

Now there were staying in Jerusalem God-fearing Jews
from every nation under heaven.
Acts 2:5

ACTS 2 REPORTS THE FIRST HOURS of the church's existence as being both international and multilingual. For Luke—the urbane, European, Gentile historian—the story of the early church was meant to document how this Jewish movement from the distant frontier city of Jerusalem could become the faith comprehensive and inclusive enough for the Roman Empire and its leadership.

From a Multilingual to a Multicultural Church
We should not be surprised that the 120 believers in the upper room knew all the languages spoken at Pentecost; they came from all those places. For the first time, under the influence of the Holy Spirit, all those languages were used in worship in Jerusalem. From then on the church's worship would be multilingual in the heart of a city where one language was official but many others were spoken by the people. Finally the curse of Babel had been broken in the city. The Holy Spirit-led church can reunite peoples fractured by language; it did so in Jerusalem.

But as we shall discover in Scripture and in contemporary urban practice, the road from multilingual to multicultural is a long and tortuous journey. The earliest church was totally characterized by a surprising unity in the risen Christ. They met in private homes and in public places to worship and eat (Acts 2:42-47). They discovered that the sacred name of God revealed in the burning bush to Moses (I AM or YHWH in Ex 3:6, 14-15), so sacred it could not be pronounced, was none other than the name of Jesus. In that name they found a power to act in the city (see Acts 3). Then they studied the Hebrew hymnal afresh, found the messianic songs in the Psalms and sang them with gusto to Jesus as "the Lord's Anointed" (Acts 4:24-26; see Ps 2:2). It was a time of euphoria in the city.

In chapters 5 and 6, however, reality strikes when the church must confront two internal sins. One was theological—the deception of Ananias and Sapphira. And one was operational—the perceived discrimination against the Greek-speaking widows at the women's meal. The disciples confronted the first sin with judgment, preaching signs, wonders and suffering.

The second sin led to an astonishing change in the structure of the church—in its constitution, if you will. The earliest apostles recognized their limits, and, rather than bring a token Greek-speaker onto their official board to model sensitivity to an aggrieved ethnic group, they brought in a whole new class of seven Spirit-filled, Greek-speaking leaders and gave them both the authority and the power to operate in the crisis. The deacons did not need to number twelve because the Greeks did not have twelve significant tribes. Instead they chose seven, symbolizing a complete and perfect group.

The deacon training that followed may have been one of the greatest miracles in Acts, given the culture where Jewish men still prayed, "Thank God I am not a Gentile, a dog or a woman." The men waited on the tables of women. They served the women in the food distribution. "Who is greater," Jesus once asked, "the one who is at the table or the one who serves? Is it not the one who is at the table? But I am among you as one who serves" (Lk 22:27). It is highly instructive to notice that the "great" Stephen and Philip began their apostolic careers doing what people today sometimes call "women's work." Luke is documenting the cultural shifts and bridges that must be crossed if our churches are to detribalize and include the whole city.

Luke, the European, viewed Stephen's four-point sermon in Acts 7 as another key event in the pluralization of the church. Stephen's longest point seems to be that all the greatest acts of God happened outside Palestine, off the map of Israel, including the Red Sea deliverance. Even the sacred Torah came not from Jerusalem but from the Sinai desert. Israel's ethnocentrism and geographical patriotism were being called into question. Stephen messed with the Jews' comfortable nationalistic worldview. By the way, I should point out that many Americans share a similar nationalistic view right now, wrapping the gospel in the U.S. flag. Regrettably, the first-century Jews chose to kill Stephen the street preacher rather than change their worldview.

No More Ethnocentric Gospel

Acts 8 pushes the boundaries of ethnocentrism further with two more remarkable photographs, one in Samaria and the other in Gaza. Samaria was north of Israel, but "down" both altitudinally and socioculturally. The mixed-race Samaritans were the despised legacy of the Assyrian wars, repatriation and occupation. The Jews hated the Samaritans and built their version of an interstate highway system to go around their country. Ironically, today the Assyrians are known as Iraqis—a people that still have problems with neighbors on all sides.

Luke recorded the stories of the good Samaritan (Lk 10:25-37), the thankful Samaritan leper (Lk 17:11-19) and the ascending Christ's declaration that "you will be my witnesses in Jerusalem, and in all Judea and Samaria, and to the ends of the earth" (Acts 1:8). He may also have known the "Samaritan woman at the well" story recorded in John 4. In any case, he knew that Israel's prejudice was likely to pass on to the church, so it was important to remind them of Philip's mission trip to the Samaritans. The whole gospel is for the whole world. One does not have the right to do an end run around the nearby socially displaced peoples to go to the ends of the earth in the name of Jesus. Humanly speaking, to evangelize people you hate is an incredibly radical act. To offer the good news of forgiveness by God and reconciliation with God and with each other will pave the way for other social services.

So many urban ministers today have become totally turned off by evangelism, especially those who have historically been discriminated against. This attitude probably stems from a reaction against the prejudice and patronizing methods used in the past to "subject peoples" in the name of mission.

I am also convinced that at the root of our discomfort is our fundamental failure to distinguish between Jesus Christ and Ann Landers. As I've said before, Ann offers advice; Jesus offers news. Advice is something *we* should do. If it works, we call it good advice. Jesus, on the other hand, offers "good news," something *he* did on the cross for us nearly two thousand years ago. News does not patronize; it liberates. Hear me when I say, *Evangelism must be the front line of ministry if it is to have integrity with the poorest and most despised peoples of our planet at all times and in every place!* Through evangelism the early church put its arms around a previously despised people, baptized them and welcomed them into the church. And Philip was there at the forefront, doing crosscultural evangelism.

The African in Gaza

The second photograph in Acts 8 comes from a desert place called Gaza. Here we see Philip's encounter with the sexually altered

Ethiopian finance minister, who was traveling home from Jerusalem. This African was reading the scroll of Isaiah, the most eloquent part of the Old Testament.

Now how did this African learn to read the Isaiah scroll, and why had he come to Jerusalem? These are very important questions. I have had the privilege of leading several urban consultations in Addis Ababa, Ethiopia. Prior to my first trip, I discovered over forty references to Ethiopia in the Bible. God must really love that place! (The last time I checked, my own country still wasn't mentioned anywhere in the Bible.)

In the course of my research on Africa in the Bible, I encountered Cain Hope Felder's wonderful study of the African texts of Scripture, *Troubling Biblical Waters: Race, Class and Family in the Bible*.[1] While in Ethiopia, I had occasion to meet other scholars at work on this history. Perhaps the Ethiopian of Acts 8 was a descendant of both King Solomon and the Queen of Sheba, thousands of whom lived in Sudan and in Ethiopia for centuries and were only in recent years airlifted to Israel, where most live at this time. This would explain how the eunuch in our text learned Hebrew and why he would desire to make a pilgrimage to Jerusalem.

In Jerusalem at the temple, however, he probably encountered a sign saying, "Eunuchs need not apply." Let's be frank. Nothing is more overtly affronting to a circumcision culture than a castration culture. I think it is fair to say that eunuchs represented a very visible rejection of messianic eschatological thinking, both then and now. Truly God used the expulsion of the Hellenists from Jerusalem to fulfill the promise of Acts 1:8. As Martin Hengel reminds us, "In ancient geography, Ethiopia was the extreme boundary of the habitable world in the hot south."[2]

In Luke's marvelous account of church history, he reminds us that on the way to Europe, where his people lived, the Holy Spirit led the church to embrace and baptize a Samaritan and an African, representing the *mestizo* or mixed-racial peoples of the world. Today the church is probably growing faster in Africa then anywhere else in the world. Africa also has the fastest-growing cities in the world. Luke's model is very important for me personally as an ethnic Norwegian-American. On the way to my people, and three chapters before Cornelius, the first European in the church, Luke, reported that an African was brought into the church. Again, for Luke this is a Pentecost story remembered. The church is on the path from being multilingual to being multicultural. Acts 8 describes two historic bridges the church had to cross to get there.

Acts 9 reports the conversion of the biggest bigot in the Middle East—Saul, an accomplice at Stephen's murder (Acts 7). Ironically, God decided to retrain this Jewish superzealot in the Arab desert for three years (Gal 1:17). Does God have a sense of humor?

Peter's Second Conversion

Perhaps nothing in the first nine chapters of Acts can prepare us for Luke's most significant Pentecost surprise. It is the detailed report of the "second conversion" of the Pentecost evangelist himself, the church's leading spokesman, Peter of Galilee. It wasn't until his own crosscultural episode with Cornelius that the coin dropped and the lights came on for Peter. After all he had been through, he was still struggling with people who brought ham sandwiches to the church picnic (forgive my colloquialism). Deep down he still cared deeply about his own culture. He did not relish becoming a minority in his own church. He hadn't resolved completely his own ethnic and cultural identity.

Peter reminds me of myself and others who know the gospel and preach orthodoxy in the traditionally approved manner in our churches. He labored to achieve doctrinal correctness. Many souls, perhaps hundreds or even thousands, have turned to Christ as a result of our ministries. But deep down, like Peter, we really wish the new converts would learn to sing our songs and do ministry our way. Peter had been with Jesus and made many adjustments in word and deed over the years, but still he had become the epitome of the cultural status quo. Acts 10:34-35 reports the drastic change in his new testimony: "I truly understand that God shows no partiality, but in every nation anyone who fears him and does what is right is acceptable to him" (NRSV).

A New Minority

In 1900, 90 percent of all Christians in the whole world were white, Northern and Western in Europe and America. By 1980 the center of gravity had shifted, and now the majority of Christians in the world are nonwhite, non-Northern and non-Western. My first reaction to such statistics is to thank God and say, "The missionaries have done many things right!" My second reaction comes when I admit that most of God's people probably won't know or appreciate any of the things we thought were so important in my church or denomination. My white, male, American "stuff" is pretty marginal now. Like many, I was trained to think ministry was autobiographical. "Plant a church that looks like you, Pastor. Reach your own kind. Stop apologizing for who you are." To do that now, of course, I would have to move further and further away from our cities to find that furtive, nervous, Eurocentric, rational culture which I know so well.

I think I understand Peter, the leader. At first the church couldn't do without him, but then his narrowness stood in the way. By God's grace, Peter was "converted" finally from cultural chauvinism, ethnocentrism and even racism.

Antioch—A Multicultural Church

Finally, Luke's Pentecost story climaxes with the establishment of the Antioch church, the first city-center church. Founded by Seleucus I in 300 B.C., Antioch on the Orontes was the most famous of the sixteen Antioch cities founded in honor of Antiochus I, the father of Seleucus. The city, like the old city of Jerusalem today, was

divided into Greek, Syrian, Jewish, Latin and African sectors. It was
Hellenized and had the major north-south and east-west highways
of the empire going through it. Strabo[3] reports a large library in this
city. In 47 B.C., Julius Caesar conferred "free city" status on it, and
later Augustus made Antioch the capital of imperial Syria. A great
center of trade, commerce and scholarship, Antioch was the third-
largest city in the empire, after Rome and Alexandria, with between
500,000 and 800,000 residents.[4] The ancient historian Josephus
tells us that many Jews were part of that population.[5]

Apparently, in Antioch, people of different ethnic backgrounds
began to cross the interior walls of the city to hear the gospel and
join the church. The Jerusalem church heard about this and sent
Barnabas, the trusted Cypriot who had sold his land to purchase
food back in Jerusalem (Acts 4). When he came to this city-center
church, Barnabas built a pastoral team that consisted of

☐ Simeon the Black (an African)
☐ Lucius of Cyrene (A North African)
☐ Manean (possibly a slave of Herod's father)
☐ Saul of Tarsus (native of Asia Minor, the land bridge to Europe)
☐ Barnabas himself (from Cyprus)

So the first large city-center church we know anything about had
a five-person pastoral team from three continents. This is the climax
of Pentecost. In Jerusalem they spoke many languages; now in
Antioch they were fleshing out multiculturalism in the structure of
the pastoral team. For me the principle is profound: the local city
church staff should increasingly match the ethnicity, class and
culture of the church's members.

The first issue this church confronted was that there were hungry
people in another city nearby. The leading pastor-teachers, Paul and
Barnabas, hand carried a hunger offering to Jerusalem. The second
issue this church faced was that there were lost cities in the empire.
The church commissioned the same leading pastor-teachers to hand
carry the gospel offering to the lost cities of the Roman Empire.

Clearly, the Antioch city center-church models going out socially to the needy and spiritually to the lost with equal integrity.

The Urban Church That Invented Foreign Missions

Soon afterward, when Paul and Barnabas began traveling to plant churches in the cities of the empire, what model did they use? What did those churches look like? What did the leadership look like? I think we have some answers. Paul and Barnabas knew only one kind of church. It was a church with a powerful gospel that transcended all the enclaves of the city and drew very diverse kinds of people into discipleship and mission. Paul talks about the ethnic walls between Jew and Gentile being torn down in Christ (Eph 2:19), where, according to his metaphor, the church itself is built together, a city of strangers becoming a holy temple animated by God's Holy Spirit.

For me, and for Luke, Barnabas and Paul, what we call foreign mission is nothing more or less than the urban mission of God's church in a world where the nations have come to live in the cities, and where the mission frontiers are no longer geographically distant but rather culturally distant, right within the shadows of the spires on our buildings.

18
WHEN TRUTH & LOVE COLLIDE

THE MISSION TRIP WITH PAUL, BARNABAS & JOHN MARK (ACTS 13; 16:36-40)

When Barnabas and Saul had finished their mission,
they returned from Jerusalem, taking with them John,
also called Mark. . . . John left them to return to Jerusalem.
Acts 12:25; 13:13

OVER THE YEARS I'VE READ much wonderful scholarship on the urban mission journeys of Paul, from Ramsay's *Cities of Paul* and *St. Paul: Traveler and Roman Citizen* to the Wayne Meeks-era literature on the social realities of Roman cities.[1]

But it is to a veteran missionary to India named E. Stanley Jones that I am indebted for an insight into the mission conflict that nearly split the early church and indeed separated Paul and Barnabas in the process.

I can imagine why someone urged the two ministry veterans to take a bright young colleague (John Mark) on the journey. Especially if he was the same young man whose mother hosted the Last Supper and who slipped out wrapped in his bedsheet to follow the disciples to the garden, only to be nabbed (Mk 14:51-52) and then escape in the buff under the cover of darkness. Perhaps his family was a donor to the mission. Who knows; it happens all the time.

Whatever the original motivation was for John Mark to travel with Paul and Barnabas, in the end he couldn't take the rigorous discipline of the trip and apparently left his elder colleagues in the lurch. Paul refused to give him a second chance and took Silas on the second journey. Barnabas took John Mark off to a separate mission in Cyprus.

Barnabas the Mentor

Barnabas is mentioned twenty-two times in Acts. He seems to be the glue of the early church. His name, "son of consolation," points out his gift and role in the body of Christ. He was a healer. He felt and acted on his feelings. He was the architect of the Antioch church and recruited Paul for public leadership after Paul had all but disappeared for five years. Clearly no one else would have required so much grace or had more that needed forgiving among early Christians than Saul (called "Paul"). Barnabas alone could risk embracing him, and he did. He recognized Paul's brilliance and created a support staff where Paul could be protected and shine as part of the Antioch pastoral team.

Luke has already reminded us that the other apostolic giant, Peter, had lingering flaws. So did Paul. The man who could applaud the execution of Stephen for heresy still had a rather short fuse—an intolerance for deviance, I suspect, theological and perhaps even operational.

Many times over the years I've had meetings in Cyprus, mostly with Middle-East Christians from Damascus, Jerusalem, Amman (ancient Philadelphia), Alexandria, Cairo and with the Antiochenes whose leaders now reside in Damascus. Since Barnabas is my own apostolic favorite, I've driven, walked and even mopeded around Cyprus meditating on his life and wondering where exactly it was he went about discipling John Mark.

E. Stanley Jones identifies Paul and Barnabas as truth and love apostles.[2] For Paul, the central truths of the faith meant everything. He had a hard time accepting doctrinal or lifestyle pluralism on the mission team. Asked about Mark, he might have said, "Oh, that quitter!" Were the same question asked of Barnabas after his impassioned sermon, he'd doubtless have replied, "Oh, thank you for asking about my cousin, John Mark. Let me tell you about grace."

Writes Jones, grace and truth are two sides of the gospel, and they belong together in the church and in the mission. But, under pressures, sometimes truth and grace come unglued and part company to become enemies, sometimes even mortal enemies.

The conflict between the North African bishop Cyprian and the Roman Presbyter Novatian (after A.D. 258) became an open battle over the issue of whether the church should forgive and welcome back into fellowship those who had "lapsed" under pressure. Novatian revered brave-unto-death Stephen, had a high view of truth and felt the integrity of the church was at stake. Only one standard could apply. Lapsing was an unpardonable sin.[3] But Cyprian reminded everyone that Peter himself, founder of the church, denied Christ three times under pressure, and that all the earliest disciples forsook Jesus under pressure and fled.

In North African cities truth and love actually became competitive denominations. It was more important to tear other believers down than to reach out to the lost.

Love Churches Versus Truth Churches

For more than three decades I've watched as today's versions of "love" and "truth" churches compete for members and influence. It is very sad, but I understand that it happens. I have made the vow never to disparage any church or its leadership in public, be it liberal or conservative. For whether true or not, Satan has a nasty habit of using such talk to further divide Christ's already fractured body and discredit the gospel in our city of mostly unchurched folks.

And now the good news! The "rest of the story" of Paul, Barnabas and Mark comes from several widespread sources.

Paul writes to the Colossians some years later regarding his trusted colleagues in Rome: Tychicus, Onesimus, Aristarchas, Mark the cousin of Barnabas, Justus, Epaphras, Luke and Demas. These kingdom workers are serving under the scrutiny of the Roman Empire (Col 4:7-14). Notice that Mark is among them—apparently with a letter of reference from Paul! "You have received instructions about him; if he comes to you, welcome him" (v. 10). After Barnabas "rehabbed" him, Mark made it to Rome to serve Paul.

In the early second Christian century, the church father Papias, a student of the apostle John, told us that Mark wrote "Peter's gospel as he preached it."[4] That explains the action orientation and eyewitness phrases in the book we call the Gospel of Mark in the New Testament.

Now most of us would be content with giving service to the two giants Peter and Paul in Rome in their old age and until their respective martyrdoms. But Mark didn't rest in Rome. He made another missionary journey in about A.D. 67. By that time Paul, Peter and perhaps Mark's older cousin Barnabas had died. Mark went to Alexandria, Egypt, and planted the gospel there.[5] Today more than 80 percent of the twelve million or so Christians in the Middle East are Egyptian, the spiritual descendants of St. Mark the martyred missionary—once young John Mark, student intern of Barnabas in Cyprus.

I get to Cairo occasionally, and when I do, I always go to St. Mark's Cathedral, the central church of the Coptic (Egyptian) Christians, to the crypt under the altar where stands the tomb of St. Mark. Each time I'm there in the quietness, I thank God for Barnabas, who didn't give up on this man who failed on his first mission trip. I also think of the many people who didn't give up on me over the years. Some years ago my oldest son, Woody, bought me a beautiful little dog. He told me, "I've named him Barnabas so he can be a comfort to you in your old age!" I have both a high view of the apostle and very fond memories of the dog who carried the name Barnabas.

19
WITH PAUL ON
AN URBAN JOURNEY
(ACTS 15—19)

One night the Lord spoke to Paul in a vision:
"Do not be afraid; keep on speaking, do not be silent.
For I am with you, and no one is going to attack
and harm you, because I have many people in this city."
Acts 18:9-10

MISSION ALWAYS RAISES A NEW agenda for the church. The expanding map requires a reexamination of old issues. Acts 15 reports the first of what today we might call a Conference on the Gospel and Culture.

As mentioned earlier, classical church history focuses on the centers of power—the three *c*'s of canon; creeds; church structures and personalities. This type of exploration provides the historian with a kind of telephone directory of the past. Williston Walker at Yale for many years was such a historian.[1] By contrast, Kenneth Scott Latourette, also a historian at Yale, was a layman who lived in China for a time; he tended to write history from the "frontier perspective." The different vantage points make it sometimes seem that these are separate histories.[2]

It is possible to examine Acts 15 and see an ecclesial struggle over power and authority in the church. But for Luke the primary issues are about the relationship of the gospel to its communication process and the traditions for developing an understanding of that gospel.

The scandal of the Christian faith is that Jesus became a real person and spoke with a local accent. As Jesus takes up residence in our lives, our most intimate communion with him always takes on local color, language, values and lifestyle. The universality of Jesus Christ is real, of course, but so are our precious enculturated "habits of the heart" in our devotion and service.

Issues of Love, Issues of Faith
I like Martin Luther's exegesis of Acts 15, which I discovered some thirty years ago. Written rather late in his life (in 1539; he died in 1546), this extended essay was called "On Councils and the Churches."[3] The Acts 15 council was the first of seven so-called ecumenical early-church councils Luther examined. Luther observed that every generation in the church's history must attempt to maintain integrity in witness, examining first what is the gospel, then what is not the gospel. For him, the gospel issues are the faith issues. They are timeless truths, but they tend to get tangled up in what Luther called the "love" issues, the local issues of culture.

For Luther, the food and Jewish calendar questions are love issues; they have nothing to do with faith or the gospel. Love issues are important, of course. We may wish to observe them, not because they are so important to the gospel, but because we wish to keep peace and harmony among our brothers and sisters in Christ. Put simply, my hair and clothing styles are not gospel issues. On the other hand, you may think your hair and clothing styles have everything to do with the gospel. They are your heritage; you value them. Well, I value you, and so I may choose to drop my tradition and follow yours because our relationship and unity are important. I'm free to conform to you, according to Luther, because the issue itself is so unimportant—it's purely cultural, a love issue.

So while we have opinions on everything, we won't *die* for everything. If Luther is right about this, periodically every church, and probably every extended family or multigenerational family, needs to sort through their own faith and culture issues so they know both how to live and what to die for should the need arise.

The Journey

No sooner had the church sorted out this issue than Paul embarked on his second urban mission journey. What follows will be a veritable jet trip with Paul. Many of us have built our theology on Paul; I argue that it's time to build our mission strategy on Paul as well. The late missionary historian Stephen Neill wrote that the early church was fortunate to have Paul as the architect of its mission because he was multilingual, bicultural and from the fair-sized city of Tarsus.[4] E. M. Blaiklock writes, in the preface to his *Cities of the New Testament,* that "Paul followed the contours of the urbanized Roman empire."[5] It seems very significant to an urban minister like me that Paul never approached a city the same way twice. He custom-made his approach. Today we call it "contextualization." He varied the three *m*'s—the message, the meeting place and the methodology—to better reach the different audiences of those cities. We will use Luke as our "tour guide."

Women in Leadership

In Philippi (Acts 16), an upper-class suburb named for Philip of Macedon, the father of Alexander the Great, Paul built his own evangelistic work on the preexisting prayer group led by Lydia, an upper-class professional woman (v. 14). Later, Paul's converts appear to have been added to Lydia's house church (v. 40). Paul's male converts were not told to replace Lydia in leadership, and when Paul later wrote to the Philippians the most joyous of his letters, he urged two women leaders, Euodia and Syntyche (female names) to agree in the Lord and asked "yokefellow" (a masculine colleague) to help these women who had ministered with him (Phil 4:2-3).

I find it interesting that the Philippian church, apparently Paul's first European church, was founded with women in leadership—colleagues of Paul in ministry. No silence, submission or coverings are mentioned here. It wasn't an issue. These were professional women who exercised power and authority in their city. To have said they couldn't lead in church would have been countercultural for Paul. For good reason he has been called "the apostle of liberty" or the "apostle of the heart set free."

Ministry to the Scholars

Athens (Acts 17) was like Paris or Boston: a cultural and educational capital. Political power had long since passed to Rome. So when Paul visited Athens, he did a museum tour. He studied sculptures and monuments as other Greek scholars would have done; then he went to the scholars' place on Mars Hill, lectured and, in the process, quoted Greek poets.

When I read A. T. Robertson's essay on Paul at Mars Hill, I noted especially the three kinds of responses to his evangelistic appeal: some mocked, some believed, some said they'd think about it.[6] Paul's handling of the scholars reminds me of Jesus' approach to Nicodemus, tantalizing him with images of new birth and wind, then patiently waiting until his own death for the conversion, perhaps three years later. The evangelism of scholars will require patience. Few will see the results.

A few years ago John Stott spoke in the Chicago area and suggested that today's university students offer a new challenge to Christian apologetics and evangelists. Today's students do not so much doubt the historicity or basic facts of Jesus Christ and the Bible; they just doubt that any first-century Palestinian Jew would have any relevance at all to us who live twenty centuries later. Students today require a lifestyle or values-driven apologetic. There is no longer a Renaissance-admiring, left-brained rational culture on the urban campus. Paul gives us the permission to adjust.

Ministry on the Docks

Corinth (Acts 18) is the classic blue-collar, commercial seaport city, five miles long, situated between two harbors on the Aegean peninsula. Ships would unload their cargo at one end of the city, transport it through the city and reload to save days of treacherous sailing around the unpredictable seas there. The glory of Corinth, however, had passed. The city had been nearly destroyed in the previous century.

The church in Corinth had contentious leaders that competed for power. Paul corresponded several times with this church, addressing this power struggle and the many problems caused by converts who tried to follow Jesus but brought along old habits and tolerated much immorality.

Paul decided to support himself in Corinth by "tentmaking" rather than taking a clerical salary. "Tentmaking" was leather working, still one of the most strategic vocations in a Greek city. Leather workers bought hides from rural farmers and employed craftspersons to make them into clothes, shoes, furniture, carpets, harnesses and of course those portable motels we call tents. These goods were then sold, and of course upper-class people were among the buyers.

Corinth was also known for its Corinthian games. In order to share the gospel with the Corinthians, Paul spiced up his message with athletic or other metaphors that the Corinthians would recognize (see 1 Cor 9:24-27).

In Ephesus (Acts 19) Paul wanted to reach Jews, so he used the rabbinic method, arguing from the covenants and promises of God in the past. Read Romans in one sitting, with its more than ninety quotes from and allusions to the Old Testament, and you'll get an idea of how Paul talked in the Ephesus synagogue until he was physically removed.

Then Luke says Paul rented the lecture hall of Tyrannus, every day for two years, from the fifth to the tenth hour (11 a.m. to 4 p.m.—see the well-attested footnote on the text of Acts 19:8-10 in most Bibles). Paul is said to have used dialogue style in the lecture hall or small Greek amphitheater (*scholē*) there. You reach Jews in synagogues and Greeks in theaters. We should not be surprised when Paul shifts the venue to reach a totally different group in the city.

City as Amplifier

When Luke reports that "all the Jews and Greeks who lived in the province of Asia heard the word of the Lord" (Acts 19:10), he is not saying that everyone in Asia heard, but that the gospel was heard all over Asia. Paul penetrated the city; the gospel did the traveling. The city has always functioned like the woofer and tweeter of an amplifying system. For the first time in American history (as of 1990) more than 50 percent of all Americans live in thirty-nine metro areas of more than one million persons. Clearly, we need more than ever to learn from Paul how to penetrate cities.

Acts 28 tells us that Paul rented a house in Rome at his own expense for two years while under house arrest. During this time his six associates—Tychicus, Epaphroditus, Aristarchus, Lukas, Demas and Marcus—worked the streets.

All six colleagues have Greek or Asian names. Apparently Paul moved into South/Asian Rome rather than Latin Rome. The city by this time had become the "catch basin" for the empire's many people, and Paul evangelized with a "reach out" team strategy.

I think Paul's urban evangelistic strategy, as reported by Luke, establishes the fact that Paul approached each city (including others like Thessalonica that we haven't looked at) very creatively and appropriately.

Paul gives me permission to do the same. I've spent many hours over the years in more than two hundred cities on six continents, looking around and asking myself, "What would Paul do here?" My late evangelism professor Paul Little used to say, "Evangelism is scratching people where they itch in the name of Jesus."[7] Certainly the apostle Paul, more than anyone else in the early church, knew that and practiced it well.

20
TWO LETTERS, TWO
URBAN SPIRITUALITIES
(PHILIPPIANS & COLOSSIANS)

Being confident of this, that he who began
a good work in you will carry it on to completion
until the day of Christ Jesus.
Philippians 1:6

He is the image of the invisible God,
the firstborn over all creation.
For by him all things were created:
things in heaven and on earth, visible and invisible,
whether thrones or powers or rulers or authorities;
all things were created by him and for him.
He is before all things, and in him all things hold together.
Colossians 1:15-17

OVER THE YEARS I'VE HAD a great deal of fun doing an experimental
Bible study using Philippians and Colossians. Dividing my audience
of ministers, missionaries and seminary people into two groups, I
give them the following instructions.

To the Colossians group I say, "Read Colossians through, imagining for now that this one book is your whole Bible. It's all you
have. Study it together for an hour, and then come back to the whole
group and tell us what your ministries would look like in this city
if all you had were the book of Colossians." My final instructions
are to pay particular attention to the location and descriptions of
Jesus Christ in the book. I issue similar instructions to the Philippians group.

This exercise has never failed to provoke controversial and stimulating discussion. The Colossians group reports in first. They notice that Christ is the firstborn of creation and a kind of cosmic glue that holds the entire universe together. He has unmasked principalities and has literally paraded them in the streets. Christ occupies a powerful reigning position physically in heaven, manifesting the "fullness of the Deity . . . in bodily form" (2:9). He delivered us from the kingdom of darkness to the light. Jesus Christ is God's icon in the world, the image of the invisible and eternal.

The Public Spirituality of Colossians

Then the Colossians group takes this transcendent, powerful Christology and transforms it into urban action plans for the churches. They affirm Christ's lordship over all city systems and structures, so they suggest church-led strategies to take on the renewal of all systems of the city. Health care, education, banking, policing, courts, housing, transit and land use policies all come under scrutiny. Are they under the powers of darkness still? How do we liberate these systems in the name of Jesus?

This Colossian spirituality also requires us to address the ecological crises of our time, for Christ is more than Lord of the church; he's Lord of creation. This Jesus permits you and me, as it did John Calvin in sixteenth-century Geneva, to view all public institutions such as a hospital or the protective city wall as gifts of "common grace" (not "saving grace").

Both are important for all citizens. Healthy persons need healthy families; healthy families need healthy communities; healthy communities make up a healthy city. For Calvin and other reformers, our tax money provides for the common-grace government institutions that God institutes for us all, not just for believers. Our tithe money provides for saving-grace institutions, such as churches or specialized mission agencies. Both taxes and tithes are the public responsibilities of Christians who are both citizens of earth and citizens of heaven simultaneously.

With blessing from the Colossian Scriptures, we can mobilize to reform city schools and health-care systems. We can work for justice in the courts of law and demand policies that are fair for all, especially the most vulnerable people in our society. We can engage in all these strategies in the name of our risen and reigning Lord whose kingdom has come, but not in its fullness. We must acknowledge that some sins have been written into law, and we must take the time to build strategies and forge coalitions to force change. We believe in sin; therefore, we know perfection will not be possible. But progress often is.

This spirituality finds its roots in the grand prophetic texts like Isaiah 58; 61—65. Using this approach, a church's growth is measured not by numbers of adherents but by the societal consequences and social transformations wrought by its members.

The Personal Spirituality of Philippians

The Colossians group is ready to go on talking about the implications of their Colossian theology, but I cut them short so the Philippians group can respond. Now the Philippians group gets very nervous as they hear all this. You see, they have noticed in Philippians that Jesus left power behind for entrance into the world. This group will almost inevitably come back to our discussion with elaborate city schemes for personal and mass evangelistic witness and detailed plans for new church planting. Frankly, this is about all they've seen that Philippians permits or requires them to do in any city while they wait for God to raise them up in the last days in glory, with our rewarded and faithful Savior Jesus Christ.

Now comes the fun. Which book is right? The group struggles to affirm both.

Question: "How far apart are these spiritualities in your Bible?" Answer: "Side by side." To which I want to extrapolate a line from the traditional marriage service, "What God has brought together, let no one put asunder."

The problem is that early on in the twentieth century, especially after 1920, the "Philippian Christians" and "Colossian Christians" separated, and a great gulf appeared. We've called it the fundamentalist-modernist controversy, and it profoundly impacted city ministry. Because modernists moved almost exclusively toward the social gospel, the fundamentalists moved toward pietism.

When Philippians and Colossians Divorced

The consequences were tragic for our cities. Whole denominations, such as the Nazarenes, Christian and Missionary Alliance and Scandinavian Free Churches were born and nurtured in nineteenth-century immigrant and slum communities. Prior to 1830 they did "revivalism and social reform," to borrow a title from Timothy Smith.[1] They did "salvation in the slums" in the late nineteenth century, according to Norris Magnussen.[2] The laity was at the forefront too, with women called to be pastors and evangelists. According to Ruth Tucker, over forty international mission agencies were also headed by women before 1910, the year of the Edinburgh Conference on world missions.[3]

Moody Bible Institute was founded in June 1886 because a woman named Emma Dryer was able both to secure D. L. Moody to back her and to convince the Fourth Presbyterian Church to give her a large start-up grant to train urban "gap" men who could stand between the churches (in the Gold Coast) and the "masses" in the ghettos. As late as 1893, William Stead published his famous book *If Christ Came to Chicago,* simultaneously with the World's Fair held in Chicago, the Columbian Exposition.[4] In his book, Stead provided several fascinating appendices. One is the list of the executive committee of Chicago's Slum Clearance Committee, chaired by a prominent Unitarian pastor. Serving with him on that same executive committee in 1893 we find this listing: R. A. Torrey, president of Moody Bible Institute.

But after 1920, the Bible institute movement became Philippian in its theology. And the best place to be a Philippian if the Colossians take over our cities is on the foreign mission field. All the energies once directed to cities were now targeted to faraway inland mission movements, most often to jungles and small towns.

Some people I know are clearly liberal theologically in the extreme; others are incredibly rigid and fundamentalist in the other extreme. I decided early on in my ministry to work for the expansion of the group who will bring Philippians and Colossians together again. As Paul said to the Romans (1:16), I will say, "I am not ashamed of the gospel, because it is the power of God." With the Colossians, I covet and pray for the lordship of Christ and the kingdom which is and which is yet to come. Of this I am sure: we will never have healthy ministry in our largest cities until we can affirm both Philippian and Colossian Christologies and the spiritualities they embody and then bring them together in the ministry of the church.

21
THE DRAMA OF NEW TESTAMENT EVANGELISM
THE STORY OF PHILEMON

Perhaps the reason he was separated from you
for a little while was that you might
have him back for good.
Philemon 15

THE SECOND-SHORTEST BOOK IN the New Testament, Philemon, is an open letter to a slaveholder near Laodicea or Colossae who also happened to be a house-church leader. I count 330 words in the Greek text, which makes it slightly longer than the Gettysburg Address of Abraham Lincoln (276 words), but it's equally dramatic.

Put briefly, the story tells about Onesimus, whose name meant "useful" or "profitable," but who apparently stole money from his master in Asia (near Laodicea) and ran away to Rome in Europe to get lost in the urban crowd. Paul, who had led Philemon to Christ in Ephesus, also reached Onesimus with the gospel in Rome a decade or so later and discipled him there. This letter to Philemon was a "cover letter" for a repatriated former slave who became an international migrant.

In order to communicate the drama of the Onesimus story, let's look at it as a five-act theater production, pulling the details together from various accounts in the New Testament.

Act I
Date: About A.D. 53
Place: Ephesus
Text: Acts 19:8-10
Paul has been evicted from the Jewish Synagogue and has rented the *scholē* (Greek amphitheater) from Tyrannus, where he presents the gospel in Socratic dialogue fashion daily for two years. Luke reports that "all Asia" hears about the gospel. Philemon, a slave-holding farmer who lives a hundred miles away near the twin towns of Colossae and Laodicea, doubtless comes to the big city often and goes to the theaters. There he hears the gospel and believes. He then returns home to plant a house church.

Act II
Date: About A.D. 54-55
Place: Laodicea
Text: Philemon 2
Philemon, Apphia and Archippus (probably Philemon's wife and son) have established a new church in their home, which would have been of considerable size (like Lydia's in Acts 16), worthy of a country gentleman or patrician farmer in the valley.

At some point Onesimus, Philemon's slave, steals money from him and takes off on a thousand-mile trek to Rome, where he becomes an urban prodigal.

Act III
Date: About A.D. 63
Place: Rome
Text: Acts 28; Philemon
At long last Paul's three missionary journeys have ended. He is now living in the European capital city, the only city in the ancient world apart from Xian, China, to exceed one million persons. The proverb said, "All roads lead to Rome"—to which I add, "and all sewers also." Cities then and now are the "catch basin" of society.

Tychicus, one of Paul's associate evangelists, may have been preaching one day in the local Lycus valley accent. This would have drawn Onesimus in, for it was his dialect. The Word reaches him and he responds. Then he enters discipleship training as a new believer under Paul and eventually joins the trusted leadership team in Rome (Col 4:9).

At some point the leaders agree that Onesimus should return to Philemon in Laodicea to seek reconciliation. They draft this letter to Philemon; it is the only personal letter we have from Paul.

After praising Philemon for his prayer and witness, Paul appeals to him to accept the runaway Onesimus back into his household. Paul calls Onesimus his "son," who now actually *is* "useful" and who now is no longer a slave but a brother in Christ.

In Philemon 15, Paul reflects theologically on this international migrant: "Perhaps the reason he was separated from you for a little while was that you might have him back for good." In other words, God brought Onesimus to the city so he could hear the gospel that brings eternal forgiveness.

This provides a larger lens through which we may view the strategic significance of the massive global migration to cities on six contents today. Like Paul, we can reflect on why God is bringing all the world to the city. Paul saw it as an opportunity for world evangelization. Perhaps God is doing the same thing today.

Paul continues by saying, "If he has done you any wrong or owes you anything, charge it to me" (v. 18). This was his polite way of saying, "Since he ripped you off, charge it to my account." Paul reminds Philemon of his line of credit in Asia: "You owe me your very self" (v. 19). Finally, Paul affirms that he knows Philemon will do much more than he asks—but mentions that he would love to use the guest room in the near future to check out how things are going. Paul ends the letter with a blessing.

The letter is rolled, sealed and hand carried a thousand miles (if they went by land).

Act IV
Date: About A.D. 64
Place: Laodicea
Text: Colossians 4:7-18

Two men, Tychicus and Onesimus, make the journey to Laodicea together, holding meetings en route, finally stopping at Colossae before moving on to Laodicea. The news of Onesimus's return travels fast. Doubtless even before they arrive, Laodicea is bustling with speculation about the situation.

Imagine that our next scene takes us to the local "Turkish" bath where slave owners play games and talk.

"Did you hear Onesimus is returning?" they whisper.

Finally someone musters up the courage to ask Philemon directly, "What are you going to do about it?" Roman law gave three options. The slave owner could brand the runaway, execute him, or purchase his freedom by buying manumission papers from the government. Execution would have probably been the normal fate for Onesimus, because according to Aristotle's slave law descriptions, slaves in that society were considered property, not people, and because Onesimus was a thief as well as a runaway. Manumission papers would not normally be purchased for a slave who committed crimes.

You can imagine the pressure on Philemon by other slaveholders. If Onesimus is freed, every slave in the region will want to run away, become a Christian and return as a brother. It will be hard to keep slaves "down on the farm," for obvious reasons. This threat was real. Read Paul's letter again, and it becomes clear which option he expected.

What happened? One thing we know: Philemon didn't tear up the letter. I think we have to assume that for the first time in history a house church was fully integrated. Some fifteen years before, Paul had written that there was no difference between slaves and free persons in Christ (Gal 3:28). But there was surely a time gap before that policy was implemented. Paul didn't ever say, "Start a church for former slaves on a side street in town." This was a historic event. The ending of slavery among Christians would eventually penetrate the larger society's consciousness.

Paul did not live to see Act IV. He died shortly after writing the letter.

Act V

Date: About A.D. 110

Place: Ephesus

Text: Ignatius of Antioch[1]

Roman soldiers have arrested Ignatius, the famous pastor of the Antioch church, and are marching him across Asia Minor to his execution. While en route and bound in chains, he writes letters to various church leaders to encourage them to keep the faith. At Smyrna he writes to the Bishop of Ephesus where Paul began ministry some fifty-seven years before. The Bishop of Ephesus to whom he writes is named . . . Onesimus.

Could it be the same Onesimus, our former slave? A. T. Robertson surveys the evidence and gives a dozen reasons why we can assume it is the same person. Other scholars agree, including Joseph A. Fitzmeyer, a current Catholic scholar.[2]

Remember his two illustrious predecessors in Ephesus? Timothy pastored there, as did the apostle John until his banishment in A.D. 96. Suppose you were on the search committee to find a suitable successor to the last living apostle—John, "the beloved disciple." After Gabriel and Michael among the angels, and Billy Graham among mortals, who could be worthy? Would you consider a former slave with a criminal record for the most prestigious pulpit in Asia?

There's more. How did this little personal letter get into the New Testament? The *Cambridge History of the Bible* says that in response to the heretic Marcion's false canon, the church was forced to collect the New Testament writings early in the second century. He suggests Ephesus as the place of its compilation.[3]

Now who do you suppose was a major figure in the collecting of our New Testament? Onesimus, of course. It makes perfect sense. He knew all Paul's associates in Rome and he led a major church in Asia. And suppose he inherited the original papyrus of this letter upon the death of Philemon. Could he not have slipped this little letter into our New Testament as the personal testimony of a slave set free—an international migrant who became a leader of the early church by the grace of God and as a testimony to urban evangelism? I call this drama in every sense of the word.

Urban Lessons from the Philemon Story

What shall we learn from the story of Onesimus in the Philemon letter? First, let us see how the gospel bounces from city to city—from Asia to Europe and back, but also from megacity to market towns. It was so then; it is so today. If we penetrate cities, the gospel will travel. Large cities are both *magnets,* drawing the nations into them, and *magnifiers,* broadcasting the gospel out into the hinterlands.

Second, let us recognize the church and parachurch partnership in urban evangelism. Paul was the evangelistic specialist. Sometimes he planted churches, but in Ephesus and Rome, two very large cities, he did not (at least not that we know about). He was the evangelist, but the fruits of his labor produced the churches, and his converts and mentors became church leaders. Here he begs the church planter Philemon to see him as a partner with him in this kingdom effort. I believe very much in specialized urban evangelism, but like Paul I see evangelism as a partnership which must be accountable to the local churches that have generalized rather than specialized ministries.

Third, we should recognize that urban evangelism will be costly business, for it's not enough to preach at the converts. Sometimes we are called on to pay twice: once because they rob us and again to train them and set them free.[4]

Fourth, we notice how radical the gospel really is after all, for it turns slaves and slave owners into family—brothers in the kingdom of God. I've heard it said that Paul didn't really address the slave issue, since in Ephesians and Colossians he told slaves to obey, to "keep their place." It's true that Paul did not organize slave revolts. Other Christians throughout history have done that. Nor did he petition the government directly—not that we know about. No, Paul knew that the church must first establish a base of kingdom values that would be a radical alternative to the life of the world.

Paul also knew that Christian slave owners had their hands on the levers of power. By living piously and ethically, leveraging their stewardship of power and resources, they would unlock the shackles of slavery. Paul knew this approach would take time. The empire was eight hundred years old; kingdom values are like slow-rising leaven. But Paul unleashed a power Rome could not squelch.

Fifth, let us understand why we need this book as we move to the close of the twentieth century, which has been called "the century of the homeless." Remember, we are witnessing the greatest migration in human history. Hemispheres are blending, and cities are filling up and growing. Only 9 percent of the earth's population lived in cities in 1900; by the year 2000 about 50 percent of our more than six billion people will be in urban centers. Since the earth is the Lord's (Ps 24:1), these statistics are not a surprise to our God. This story lets us see what can happen for world evangelization when migration occurs. God is moving the earth around.

New Neighbors

Paul's reflection on Onesimus's migration in Philemon 15 gives us a special lens to watch Asian evangelization today. The Chinese, Japanese, Koreans and Indians are everywhere in the cities of the world. Like the Jews of the first century, they have moved to center stage on five or six continents. *Kairos* time, the opportune moment, is at hand. A new Pentecost spark among these immigrants and refugees could spread like wildfire and produce the greatest harvest Asia has ever seen. The leadership for the churches of Asia may, in fact, be in training now in Los Angeles, New York, Buenos Aires, London, Chicago, Vancouver, São Paulo and Toronto. Strong Asian discipleship is taking place in all these cities.

Sixth, this drama took fifty-seven years, and the original cast never saw the conclusion. This reminds me that the kingdom is both now and "not yet." We must be in urban evangelization for the long haul, not just until the grant runs out. We need this perspective because it runs counter to so many of our Western, money-driven planning and operating procedures. Cities are constantly recycling with new populations. What a tragedy that so many denominations sold out early on and now may be locked out.

Seventh, I realize that not every migrant is a potential bishop, but if I knew that fifty years from now my non-English-speaking neighbors might be Billy Grahams for China or Mother Teresas for Brazil, I know I'd get more personally involved and committed to them.

I'm impressed that Jesus poured his life into twelve and lost one. Paul at the end of his life was heavily invested in six, one of whom, Demas, did forsake him. If the city is big, large meetings may not be the best strategy—nor a hectic program schedule to match the frenetic urban calendar. I never see Paul alone in ministry. He invested in people, even though, as we know from the John Mark story, it was not always easy.

For many years I've struggled to help pastors understand the urban church-growth reality. It just can't be measured by the number of members, people in attendance or dollars in the offering. A city church of 100 can have ten or more countries in the membership. City churches are hubs, "worldwide webs" of relationships that link back to family or colleagues in sending countries where the ministry is underground or mushrooming right now.

Urban pastors also need to remember the lesson from our Middle

Eastern churches that the Great Commission is not only horizontal (nation to nation) but also vertical (generation to generation). Therefore, multigenerational faithfulness must be part of our measurement as well.

Eighth, Philemon reminds me that churches that are small, intimate and led by believers with limited pastoral training may be the very best places for training the next generation of large-city church leaders. The human-scale intimacy and generalist opportunities that these little churches offer young leaders may be why I and so many of my generation of urban church pastors came from small, rural churches. We should never assume that urban leadership must be home-grown or that leadership development is done best where the church staff is huge and highly professional. As I read the Bible, leaders from Moses to Onesimus seem to have multienvironmental experiences in all sizes of communities and ministry structures. There seems to be no one standard way of generating these leadership giants. As frustrating as it appears to educators in the "angel factories" (as I call seminaries), that's the reality of the kingdom of God.[5]

22

ETHNICITY IN THE CHURCH—IS IT STILL OKAY TO BE JEWISH?

(HEBREWS)

Instead, they were longing for a better country—
a heavenly one. Therefore God is not ashamed
to be called their God, for he has prepared a city for them.
Hebrews 11:16

I ONCE GAVE A LECTURE ENTITLED "One Thousand Years to Make Vikings into Baptists." It was the result of reflection on my own salvation history as an American Baptist of Norwegian ancestry. The roots of my story go back to Celtic and German missionaries like Ansgar, the German Bishop of Hamburg who crossed the Baltic in A.D. 834 and baptized some Swedish converts.

The earliest Viking Christians were Catholic, of course, and they tended to mix Thor with Yahweh. My roots were Catholic for nearly seven hundred years until a second German mission crossed the Baltic, this time from Wittenberg, and we became Lutherans. Then a third German mission came from Halle, and Lutheran pietism was born in Sweden and Norway. In 1848, a few furtive Swedes baptized each other and were promptly thrown in jail. Today the jail doors are displayed in the church for all to see. So 1,014 years after Ansgar, a Scandinavian Baptist Church was born.

I grew up as a Norwegian Lutheran pietist and became a Baptist in my college years. I recommitted myself to my adopted church after rather intensive studies of Baptist origins and distinctives, but scratch me and you'll find Luther, and go deeper and you might find Augustine. I have a pretty good idea where my own spiritual genes came from. Generations of faithful believers preceded me, but only a few would call themselves Baptist.

This ethnic history has given me a special appreciation for the people I've pastored over the years, many of them with colorful and wildly diverse spiritual roots. Some, of course, rejected their social origins when they came to Christ, then looked to the church to function as extended family for them. Some were cut off by family for converting to Christ in the first place.

As a lecturer on Chicago urban-church history over the years, I have long been fascinated with the Roman Catholic ethnic experience in my city. Notre Dame professor Charles Shannabruch's marvelous *Chicago's Catholics: The Evolution of an American Identity 1830-1930*[1] describes a century of ethnic strategies church leaders used, from Bishop Quarter to Cardinal Mundelein. The people who were killing each other in the Franco-Prussian War and World War I in Europe were going to church together (at times) in Chicago. While the book was a case study of what happened in Chicago, the principal lessons are useful everywhere.

The literature on ethnicity in the city is far too vast to cite here.[2] When I was a pastor, my approach was to attempt the study of one ethnic group each year in my own parish area, starting with Appalachian coal- and cotton-culture migrants. I just could not understand them in the Chicago setting. After visits to Appalachia and reading many books, I finally began to get some insight into their culture. In the meantime, my respect for their experience increased dramatically. I repeated this process for other groups over the years, but never exhaustively. I was no expert, just a pastor trying to understand my immigrant and migrant congregation.

Corean and I also adopted an African-American boy when he and our other sons were in high school. We have worked hard over the years to understand and reinforce his roots in a variety of ways.

Ethnicity in Hebrews

Now I bring this agenda into a fresh look at the New Testament book called Hebrews. Thirty-eight years ago I took a Bible class entitled "Leviticus and Hebrews." The thrust of the class was to see Hebrews as the fulfillment of Old Testament temple and priestly patterns.

I am not the artist in my family—my wife, my son and others have tutored me in this area and increased my enjoyment and understanding of art. I have listened to several Leonard Bernstein explanations of the symphonies I enjoy and have learned that a Miro sculpture has a kind of code language behind it. Yet understanding the symbolism is only part of understanding a work of art; one must also understand its context.

While my course on Hebrews years ago uncovered the meanings of symbols, it did not address the real challenges of Jewish ethnicity for those who chose to follow a Jew named Jesus into a Christian church.

I think the book of Hebrews was written much later than the Jerusalem Council of Acts 15. There, as we observed, the church sorted out faith issues from cultural or ethnic issues, summing up their conclusions in a letter written to the churches. As far as I can tell, that letter, with its instruction to honor Jewish practices such as circumcision and abstaining from certain foods, was never mentioned again.

Recently I observed some teenage Catholic girls at a local fast-food restaurant holding up their line as they argued about whether or not they were allowed to eat meat during Holy Week. They were all Roman Catholic, but their approach was not uniform. Some ate meat; some didn't. This is a new generation that doesn't remember Vatican II, when the rules changed, and often doesn't know why they changed, but many of today's generation still agonize over these cultural issues.

How Does the Spirit Work in Cultures?

In the same way, many Asian Christians struggle to honor parents while rejecting their parents' religion—and years later re-sort the issues in an attempt to accommodate their multigenerational family. I remember a seminary chapel presentation by a brilliant Korean seminary student, who reviewed 2,000 years of his history to find 1,900 years of God's activity during the pre-Christian years. This was meaningful for his spiritual map.

The writer to the Hebrews knows that Christ is the Messiah and that he fulfills all the great themes in the Jewish tradition. The author seems to be revisiting every part of that tradition and celebrating it. This is a person who is grateful to be Jewish when many, if not most, in the church were Roman or Greek or something else. The Jewish war and the battle of Jerusalem may have created the same agony in our author's spirit as Hitler's Nazism did for proud, cultured Germans. Fifty years after World War II, the essayists are still sorting through the spiritual experience of the Germans.

So, while most of the church in the first century had permission to distance their own experience from any Jewish traditions, and while others, called Ebionites, were so Jewish their Christianity was suspect, our author struggles to find an authentic ethnic spirituality. If we Gentiles take over this book and spiritualize it or reduce it to religious typologies to explain our own experience, I think we marginalize the author's own testimony. I think Hebrews is a unique book.

However (and this is my own caveat), I think Hebrews provides a model that gives permission for every other ethnic Christian to do the same thing—to identify your own spiritual map and celebrate the sovereign God's movement in your past.

A Historical Idea with a New Significance

In A.D. 787 the Western Catholic church added one word, *filioque,* meaning "and the Son," to the creed they recited every Sunday in the ancient churches. The phrase was originally "the Holy Spirit proceeds from the Father," to which they added "and the Son."[3]

The Eastern Christians were horrified, not only that historic creeds could be changed, but that Muslim neighbors might accuse Christians of having three gods. Their fears were real.

The Western Christians were surrounded by tribal Christians who tended to view Jesus as a glorified tribal chief. Their fears were real too. They thought they could amend the creed to emphasize the deity of Jesus, in order to help local Christians better see the full glory and deity of Christ.

We Westerners not only amended the creed. It has become obvious to contemporary missiologists that by adopting the word *filioque* we've helped put the Holy Spirit in a box taped shut by Christology.

What does all this have to do with making one's own ethnic map? I believe the Eastern Christians got this one right. The Holy Spirit, as they understand theology, works in every culture long before the name of Christ is known. The Orthodox missionaries would advise you to "take off your shoes" when entering another culture, because even if no church exists there, it is still holy ground—God's Spirit is present. The Orthodox are deeply charismatic and hold steadily to their Christology.

Remember how Isaiah saw God at work in Cyrus? The God of Scripture is not bound to my own denominational history or even church history as a whole. God's redemptive plans are far more cosmic than our own understanding. Please use Hebrews as a model and the unbounded Holy Spirit to guide you to map your own spiritual roots.[4]

Whenever I'm with Arab church leaders like Elias Chacour, a pastor in Galilee, I am amazed at how they relate to Muslims in their village and Jews nearby. Father Chacour knows they are all cousins; they are children of Abraham. Most of the Arabs of Palestine were Christians for centuries before they became Muslims (often under pressure). Chacour writes movingly about them in his book *Blood Brothers*.[5]

The idea of race and the identity of peoples is one of the most significant issues in our cities and indeed the world. As an urban Christian I respect unique racial, ethnic or cultural distinctives. Yet at the root I affirm that *we are all cousins*. We—Christian, Jew or Muslim—are the children of Abraham, and we must learn to live together in the city along with every tribe and nation. Nevertheless, I think it's okay for me to be a white American Baptist of Norwegian descent, married to a Lutheran who descended from a Dutch Mennonite father and a Scotch Presbyterian mother.

23
THE EMPIRE
STRIKES BACK
THE DOWNWARD SPIRAL FROM
ROMANS 13 TO REVELATION 13

*Everyone must submit himself to the governing
authorities, for there is no authority except that
which God has established. The authorities that
exist have been established by God.*
Romans 13:1

*Terrified at her torment, they will stand far off and cry:
"Woe! Woe, O great city,
O Babylon, city of power!
In one hour your doom has come!"*
Revelation 18:10

ROME WAS NEVER REALLY the ultimate goal for Paul, even though it
was the capital of the Roman Empire. In fact, Paul wrote to the
Roman Christians that he needed to cover more territory and hoped
to stop by for a season en route to Spain (Rom 15:24).

Long before I read David Bosch's brilliant missiological text
Transforming Mission: Paradigm Shifts in the Theology of Mission,[1] I
had also concluded that Paul's sense of mission urgency came in no
small part from his reading of Isaiah 66:18-22.

"And I, because of their actions and their imaginations, am about
to come and gather all nations and tongues, and they will come
and see my glory.

"I will set a sign among them, and I will send some of those who survive to the nations—to Tarshish, to the Libyans and Lydians (famous as archers), to Tubal and Greece, and to the distant islands that have not heard of my fame or seen my glory. They will proclaim my glory among the nations. And they will bring all your brothers, from all the nations, to my holy mountain in Jerusalem as an offering to the LORD—on horses, in chariots and wagons, and on mules and camels," says the LORD. "They will bring them, as the Israelites bring their grain offerings, to the temple of the Lord in ceremonially clean vessels. And I will select some of them also to be priests and Levites," says the LORD.

"As the new heavens and the new earth that I make will endure before me," declares the LORD, "so will your name and descendants endure."

For the ancient Hebrews, Tarshish (or Spain) was "Land's End," as it were. I think Paul saw Isaiah's vision of the glory of God covering the arc of all known nations. He could picture the brethren streaming back into Jerusalem from all those mountains to the Lord's holy mountain. Then he saw that the new heaven and new earth would follow. Paul was a driven man, but not by politics; he could visualize the glory of God so powerfully he could taste it. Caesar and Rome could never be the legitimate goal of mission for him.

I believe this explains in part Paul's "offering strategy." He wanted to take both money and people back to Jerusalem as an offering, a sign of his eschatological completion of God's world mission.

Leveraging Old Mother Churches

One of the great world mission strategies of the ethnic church is to send funds and human resources to assist the historic mother churches back home. One reason the 840,000 Poles living in Chicago cannot (and should not, in my opinion) totally fold into Chicago and swallow our American agenda is that God is asking them to leverage the liberation of Poland and its churches back home. This is also true for other national churches in the U.S., especially the Middle Eastern churches. Suffice it to say that this international leveraging is a major trend in urban ministry in our day, and it is fundamentally a two-thousand-year-old idea we got from Paul.

While Paul respected Rome, he was not cowed by the empire. Romans 13 shows a rather optimistic and straightforward view of the government. Governments have limited but important powers, delegated by God (13:1). Implicit, of course, is the idea that Christians are to be careful judges of whether governments—be they city, regional, national or international—exceed their divine right to power and authority. Paul really meant it when he said, "Rulers hold no terror for those who do right" (13:3), but that was before he died at the hands of that same government. Nero was bad enough, but John had to face Domitian's misappropriations of power, and that was far worse.

One advantage of attending seminary during the Vietnam era in the late sixties was that there was a raging debate about the nature and limits of government. This sharpened my sense of the issues. At one point, I thought about writing an essay called "The Three Richards in my Life"—Richard J. Daley was my mayor, Richard Ogilvie was my governor and Richard Nixon was my president. I disagreed on various policy and ethical issues with all of them, regardless of their political party.

The Limits of Governmental Structures

Oscar Cullman's writings, *Christ and Time* and especially *The State in the New Testament,* helped me see the limits of government.[2] Like Barth and Brunner, Cullman wrote under the lingering cloud of World War II when all optimism was checked by the Cold War and the new atomic age. Cullman helped me see that the Roman government changed between Romans 13 and Revelation 13. During those three decades, the church changed its attitude toward the government under Rome's demonically driven usurpation of divine power. The social world of Paul and the social world of the seven churches of Revelation were "worlds apart." A dramatic shift had occurred.

By the end of the first century, the cities of Asia had become bastions of Greco-Roman culture and ready hosts for the Imperial Cult of Domitian. S. R. F. Price puts it like this:

> The imperial cult, like other civic cults, was tied up with the political, social and economic structures of the contemporary world whose ideals and conflicts were articulated through it. Except for the resistance of Christians to festivals in honor of the emperor, the conflicts within the cities and between cities took place within a framework that was shared by all. The struggles of competition to win at the imperial games, the fighting for honorific positions by the local elites and the concern for the standing of one's own city against other cities for the province all presupposed (and enhanced) the importance of the imperial cult. The cult thus helped to ensure that the energies of the subjects of Rome were not directed toward subversive activities. It was a force for order, rather than disorder, and consolidated the social and political hierarchies from which it arose.[3]

The steady trend was the centralization of power in an emperor, including the dominance of local elites over the populace, cities over other cities, and Greek over indigenous cultures. As the cities prospered, the churches were repressed by an intolerant empire.

Under such intense pressure the church retreated to apocalyptic language and developed the technicolor symbolism we see in the book of Revelation. Both 2 Peter and Jude reveal the same tension. The churches were disparate, reeling from dissension within and persecution without. Christian leaders were banished, tortured and killed by this increasingly totalitarian state.

C. J. Hemer has suggested that the seven churches of Revelation 1—3 were more than symbols. They may also have served as postal centers for the region as a whole, in which case the book of

Revelation would have been intended not only for them but also for others.[4]

So the *benign* Rome Paul knew had become the *beastly* Rome of John. Yet the city churches addressed in Revelation are not blameless or beyond critique. Even though Christ sympathized with their suffering, he made it clear that to compromise the gospel under pressure is still inexcusable. And so every church was warned, and all but the Laodicean Church were also praised for their struggles to be faithful under pressure.

Two Trees: Different Symbols

My home state, Washington, is known for its forests containing the huge, straight, tall Douglas Fir, the official state tree. Indeed these trees are awesome (and increasingly rare). My own favorite tree, though, is the Alpine that grows way up near the snow pack of the mountains. For a couple of months in the summer it blooms beautifully, in spite of its gnarled trunk and limbs and its scraggly root system. The other ten months of the year it bears huge weights of melting snow and moving ice. I marvel at the way it survives and blooms for a season.

These heroic trees remind me of the Middle Eastern churches—Orthodox, Catholic, Protestant and evangelical. It is so easy, as Westerners often do, to point out the idiosyncrasies in doctrine, dress and practice, and even their competition among themselves in the face of centuries of hostile pressures. I am not Orthodox, but I got most of my doctrine from them via Europe. I truly admire them and love to be with them.

I can understand the Orthodox use of icons and symbols, and even their use of archaic languages, because I've read the book of Revelation. The Ethiopian church worships in the ancient Gese language, not Amharic, the official Ethiopian language. The Russians use old Slavonic; the Egyptians, immersed in a sea of Arabic speakers, use old Copt—and, yes, American blacks use Shakespearean English, the King James Version. I understand this. It is their prayer language; it is also a code language.

Let me explain. Suppose a member of the Roman Gestapo had come into the First Baptist Church of Thyatira and heard the preacher talking about Babylon this and Babylon that. *Bizarre!* he might think. *They're more out of it than I thought. Hasn't anyone told them Babylon went out of business centuries ago?* Yet by speaking against Babylon instead of Rome, the church was protected from charges of rebellion. In the same way, the American black church did not talk about the underground railroad. They sang "Swing Low, Sweet Chariot," and everybody except the slave owners knew what they meant.

The theology of Revelation is phenomenal, as I've learned from R. H. Charles and so many others over the years.[5] But from my urban parish vantage point, I see something else going on in Revelation. I see that churches under pressure still retreat to code language in worship, something they must do while family and loved ones stay behind in the old country.

The oldest churches in Christendom are my newest neighbors here in Chicago. It's probably not so important that they learn my language. I still live near Romans 13. It is far more important that I learn their prayer and worship language, for they have lived closer to Revelation 13 for centuries.

24
SO LONG, BABYLON, I'LL MISS YOU
(REVELATION 14—18)

I saw the Holy City, the new Jerusalem,
coming down out of heaven from God,
prepared as a bride beautifully dressed
for her husband.
Revelation 21:2

THROUGHOUT THE BIBLE, BABYLON IS a symbol of the city which is anti-God. Literally the name means "gate to God." The Babylonian disease leads a city to build towers that breach heaven's gates. "Move over, God, we're coming up" might be their motto. Lucifer (Is 14:12-20) would have made a great Babylonian.

Babylon was also the destroyer of Jerusalem, its temple and monarchy. Babylon was a city the Jews hated for good historical reasons. Two New Testament passages refer to the historic city of Babylon, located on the Euphrates river, some eighty miles southeast of today's city of Baghdad in Iraq (see Mt 1:11, 17; Acts 7:43). But in 1 Peter 5:13 and in Revelation Babylon is the code name for Rome, capital city of the Roman Empire.

The 1 Peter text applies the exile metaphor to the church, for Christians were dispersed throughout Rome as Jews had been in ancient Babylon. Revelation goes further in fleshing out the metaphor.

Revelation teaches that history will climax in a battle between two titans, the earthly city of Babylon and the heavenly city of Jerusalem. St. Augustine didn't invent the idea of two competing kingdoms, though he wrote of it most brilliantly in *The City of God.*[1] The Charles Dickens classic *A Tale of Two Cities* (Paris and London) picks up the theme, as do theologians like Walter Rauschenbusch and Reinhold Niebuhr with their two-kingdom discussions.[2] Recently in Washington, D.C., I heard Pastor Gordon Cosby of the Church of the Savior discuss the discipleship process. He said that early in his ministry he was naive and thought that one could develop a Christian worthy of church membership in six months. Now he has conceded that it takes a minimum of two years, because what's involved in following Jesus is nothing less than "switching kingdoms."

The epic battles of bowls and plagues described in Revelation are somewhat like modern alien movies. The bad guys keep returning to fight in new sequels every two or three years as the film technology improves. Don't be alarmed. We've read the last chapter. We know how this one turns out. We win!

My late friend Bill Leslie, a long-time Chicago pastor, once gave our Chicago Network this illustration. Because his church duties often extended late into Sunday afternoon, he used to miss many Chicago Bears football games. (Like all sons of coaches and former athletes, he was a real fan—name your sport.) On the way home, he would hear the final score. Later, watching a taped telecast of the game, he would find himself all tied up in sweaty emotional knots when the Bears would look bad or fall behind. Then he'd catch himself and say, "But we won! I already know that!" We know the final score in the game of two kingdoms: the game is actually over, but it's still playing out.

Jacques Ellul was greatly impressed by the Babel and Babylonian texts in the Bible. Like many, I grabbed his book *The Meaning of the City* when it came out in 1968.[3] Like C. S. Lewis, Ellul was not a professional theologian, but he has had a profound effect to this day on the way many Christians think about cities in Scripture. Put simply, Ellul views Babylon as the archetype of evil in Scripture and concludes that all cities are evil. I personally think Ellul misread the data. The Bible has many other city case studies he could have used to correct his rather depressing view. As I have said elsewhere, Cox's *Secular City* was too optimistic in 1966;[4] Ellul was too pessimistic in 1968.

I love writers from whom I can glean aphorisms or pithy descriptive phrases. William Temple gave me one: "Heresies are exaggerations of truths." Babylon exaggerated the good and evil all cities contained then and contain now.

The Towering Inferno

Have you ever been to a big urban fire? I saw 1,400 fires in my parish in 1973, 400 fires in one summer of gang violence and arson-for-profit schemes. Twenty-seven members of my church had their houses burn that year. I didn't see Beirut burn, though I was there in 1976 when the civil war began and again when it ended in 1994. I saw the devastation caused by fire in that city. More recently we see the intentional burning of black American churches.

No, I don't chase fire engines, but follow me to the urban fire to end all fires in Revelation 18. Standing in the crowd, you can hear a cacophony of noises: the roar of engines on the ground, helicopters overhead, flames, steam, shouts from firefighters amid blaring radio and walkie-talkie squawk boxes. At night the darkness and acrid smoke add to the confusion. Looking through the crowd you can see the city up close and in your face. Some people are nasty, while others scream in terror. Most are just sullen and sober. A few weep.

Someday the angels of God will torch Babylon (Rome and Chicago), and I try to imagine myself in the crowd when the fire hits home. The blaze spreads from neighborhood to neighborhood until it reaches mine. My house, my street, churches, schools, doctor's office, grocer—all are gone. All my stuff—the things I've accumulated, the places I've frequented—they're all gone.

Then I realize the city's world-class symphony hall is ablaze. The wonderful museums, offices, factories, airports, phones, faxes, television, radio, libraries are all gone.

The shops! What about the shops? Over sixty nations live in our square mile. We have everything here. It's beautiful. There's the old-world cobbler who still fixes kids' ripped baseball gloves for fifty cents. Gone! Suddenly it occurs to me, *I'm dependent on this city. I can't live without it.*

How can I be a famous, successful urban minister if my city is taken away? *O God, don't do this to me. I need my Babylon!* Gone. Now I am weeping (Rev 18:15) along with all the others. Everything we know and love and need is gone. No symphony, no weddings, no parties (18:21-23); only silence and emptiness.

Then, just when I give up hope that anything has survived, I faintly hear a distant choir. For thousands of years heaven's choirs have rehearsed the Hallelujah Chorus for this very moment (Rev 19). No one has to tell me to stand; I am standing. The parade has begun and here it comes, down my street. Will somebody call for television coverage? The Rose Parade was never like this. Where did these floats come from?

The conflict between the kingdoms culminates with judgment. The Nuremberg trials at the end World War II were dramatic, but this is *Dead Man Walking* big-time, multiplied by casts of thousands.

Now it is all over and we all live happily in a rebuilt Garden of Eden, right? A nice, rural, ranch-type house will do for me, thank you. "God has been planning this for *how* long?" I ask.

"Since before the foundation of the world," comes the response. I stretch to see. Jesus told us he'd be building a place (Jn 14:1-4), as Isaiah had told centuries earlier (Is 65:17-25).

So what is it? All history is on its tiptoes awaiting God's surprise.

The trumpet sounds, the curtain opens and it's . . . it's . . . it's . . . *another city!* An urban future forever. And what a city it is! I get the tour (Rev 21—22), which ends with the promise "I am coming soon" (22:20).

"Amen, Lord Jesus, come soon!" I respond. In the meantime I hear the benediction, "The grace of the Lord Jesus be with God's people. Amen" (22:21). The expanded Hebrews 11 crowd is in the stands. The seven churches of Revelation 1—3 are in honored box seats down front.

So long, Babylon, I'll miss you. But not for long. God's new city is coming! I have hope.

25
THE URBAN
FAMILY ALBUM

Therefore, since we are surrounded by
such a great cloud of witnesses . . .
let us run with perseverance the race
marked out for us.
Hebrews 12:1

BAPTIST THEOLOGIAN BERNARD RAMM WROTE a book called *Witness of Spirit*, which I read in 1963, shortly after it was published.[1] I had always liked learning history, but Ramm gave me some theological reinforcement for taking history more seriously and incorporating it into my spirituality.

The Holy Spirit has been gifting the church with leadership continuously and building up Christ's body since the first century. I'd always seen Paul's description of the gifts of the Spirit in Ephesians 4:11-15 as a present-tense reality—that as a pastor I was to build up the body for its ministry. Ramm reminded me that to ignore the Holy Spirit's gifts at any time or place in history was a not-very-subtle way of blaspheming the Spirit and denying the gift of teaching in the church. The Spirit's work is cumulative as well as a breakthrough experience.

In the spirit of Matthew chapter 1, I'd like to show you my urban family photo album, where you can meet a few of those who have been my historical support group for several decades. Granted, this look will be a bit superficial, but it's really capable of infinite expansion. Let's open this album together.

The Soul of the City (Second Century)

In about A.D. 140, a letter was written to a government official telling him that Christians were not a threat to the city—rather, they were the conscience or very soul of the city. This anonymous "Letter to Diognetus" gives us a beautiful snapshot of how early Christians, as citizens of cities, viewed the role of the church in the world. I will quote the entire section, so you can see all the detail in this photograph:

> For Christians cannot be distinguished from the rest of the human race by country or language or customs. They do not live in *cities* of their own; they do not use a peculiar form of speech; they do not follow an eccentric manner of life. This doctrine of theirs has not been discovered by the ingenuity or deep thought of inquisitive men, nor do they put forward a merely human teaching, as some people do. Yet, although they live in Greek and barbarian *cities* alike, as each man's lot has been cast, and follow the customs of the country in clothing and food and other matters of daily living, at the same time they give proof of the remarkable and admittedly extraordinary constitution of their own commonwealth. They live in their own countries, but only as aliens. They have a share in everything as citizens, and endure everything as foreigners. Every foreign land is their fatherland, and yet for them every fatherland is a foreign land. They marry, like everyone else, and they beget children, but they do not cast out their offspring. They share their board with each other, but not their marriage bed. It is true that they are "in the flesh," but they do not live "according to the flesh." They busy themselves on earth, but their citizenship is in heaven. They obey the established laws, but in their own lives they go far beyond what the laws require. They love all men, and by all men are persecuted. They are unknown,

and still they are condemned; they are put to death, and yet they are brought to life. They are poor, and yet they make many rich; they are completely destitute, and yet they enjoy complete abundance. They are dishonored, and in their very dishonor are glorified; they are defamed, and are vindicated. They are reviled, and yet they bless; when they are affronted, they still pay due respect. When they do good, they are punished as evildoers; undergoing punishment, they rejoice because they are brought to life. They are treated by the Jews as foreigners and enemies, and are hunted down by the Greeks; and all the time those who hate them find it impossible to justify their enmity. To put it simply: *What the soul is in the body, that Christians are in the world. The soul is dispersed through all the members of the body, and Christians are scattered through all the cities of the world.* The soul dwells in the body, but does not belong to the body, and the Christians dwell in the world, but do not belong to the world. The soul, which is invisible, is kept under guard in the visible body; in the same way, Christians are recognized when they are in the world, but their religion remains unseen. The flesh hates the soul and treats it as an enemy, even though it suffers no wrong at their hands, because they rage themselves against its pleasures. The soul loves the flesh that hates it, and its members; in the same way, Christians love those who hate them. The soul is shut up in the body, and yet itself holds the body together. The soul, which is immortal, is housed in a mortal dwelling; while Christians are settled among corruptible things, to wait for the incorruptibility that will be theirs in heaven. The soul, when faring badly as to food and drink, grows better; so too Christians, when punished day by day, increase more and more. It is to no less a post than this that God has ordered them, and they must not try to evade it [italics mine].[2]

Although the influence of Greek thought can be seen in this letter, the Christians clearly did not embrace the platonic desire to escape the role of the flesh in society. On the contrary, they believed God had commanded them not to evade their post.

So, a hundred years after Jesus, a Christian leader rallied believers to be the "soul of the city." What a great photograph!

An Urban Nursery (Second Century)

Bishop Samuel of Cairo relayed to me another precious photograph as he described women deacons in urban Egypt in the second century. Samuel was a brilliant Coptic scholar and teacher. He was sitting behind President Sadat at the time of his assassination in 1981 and was killed by the same hail of bullets.

Years before his death, I met with him, and he told me how Christianity spread in Egypt. He told me that in the second century, church women provided nursing mothers who sat in the public squares, often under pagan statues, while other women went up and down the streets to collect the unwanted babies abandoned in the night. They brought them, nursed, bathed and raised them.

That is one way the church grew in Egypt. The early church responded to a problem in their city—abandoned children—and developed a "baby hunt" ministry. What a marvelous photograph.[3]

Urban Garbage Collectors (First Century)

E. A. Judge and Lewis Mumford, among others, provide photos of early believers who were artisans, freedmen and slaves.[4] Other writers describe how as garbage collectors they collected and individually buried the bloated, diseased bodies people tossed into the garbage.

How did Christians get into the garbage business? Consider this quote from Mumford:

The Christian expectation of radical evil—sin, pain, illness, weakness and death—was closer to the realities of this disintegrating civilization than any creed based on the old images of "life, prosperity and health." Instead of evading the ugly realities of his time, the Christian embraced them. By doing willingly what pagans sedulously avoided, he both neutralized and in some measure overcame the forces that threatened him. He visited the sick; he comforted the widow and the orphan; he redeemed the ignominies of starvation, sickness and squalor by making them an occasion for fellowship and love.[5]

These believers allowed Christ in them to confront and transform the ugliness of their day. Their faith moved them to hunt for babies and bodies. I ask myself, *Does my theology affect my own work habits like this?*

Tertullian (Third Century)

Tertullian, the great North African lawyer, taunted the empire with these words: "We are but of yesterday, and we have filled every place among you—cities, islands, fortresses, towns, market-places, the very camp, tribes, companies, palace, senate, forum—we have left nothing to you but the temples of your gods."[6]

Early Christians penetrated the whole city, but not by claiming space for church buildings or programs of their own. They penetrated everybody else's space instead. This is an important lesson for me.

Ulfilas (Fourth Century)

Ulfilas was deemed an Asian heretic with a less than fully orthodox view of Jesus. After his banishment he became a missionary among violent Gothic peoples who had a theology of holy war. Ulfilas refused to translate the book of Kings for their Bible. He thought his people would use Kings to justify war-making.[7] I can understand his decision. How do we describe Kings to street gangs?

Benedict of Nursia (Sixth Century)

Benedict of Nursia developed a special kind of monastery sometime after A.D. 529. He organized lay folks, sent them to the worst, most violent places in Europe and organized their spirituality around work, worship, study and sleep. These monks got no outside funds from Rome. They were self-sufficient, despite being in the most bleak areas of Europe during the "dark ages." They converted Europe spiritually and created the economies in their respected regions. We especially need the gifts of the Benedictines today! I see groups like Jesus People USA as contemporary Benedictines (they're not all Catholic anymore).[8]

A Thousand Years of Uncertainty

Kenneth Scott Latourette provides a somewhat disturbing portrait of church growth. He writes that from A.D. 500 to 1500 the church did not grow. It merely exchanged real estate. We gave up Africa and gained Europe. There were about the same number of believers and the same number of square miles under Christian influence in the year 1500 as in the year 500.[9]

As I reflected on his research, it became clear that we may be doing this again in our time. But this time, we are exchanging urban churches for suburban ones.

India (Seventh Century)

Today India is situated between two Muslim bookends: Pakistan on the west and Bangladesh on the east. I knew that the whole area used to be Hindu, so during a trip to India I had the opportunity to ask a knowledgeable Muslim how Islam came to those regions. He showed me a map of the region and pointed out that the rivers cover more area in the Punjab and Bangladesh.[10] The Hindu elite had looked down upon and discriminated against the lower-caste river peoples. In the seventh century, Muslim traders sailed these rivers and began to build relationships of respect with the river peoples. Within a hundred years, both regions became entirely Muslim—not because of clerical leaders, but because of a brotherhood.

In 1994 there were seventy-three mosques in Chicago. In 1996,

I am told, the number has risen to more than 140. Many are standing where churches used to be. The power of Islam is still the brotherhood it provides, and it remains effective for Muslim evangelization, especially among peoples who have felt discriminated against by Christians.

Francis, Dominic and Innocent III (Thirteenth Century)

Francis of Assisi drew near the pope in 1210 and received official permission for the ministry of "Little Brothers" among the poor and needy of Italy. For Francis, faith was love in action on the streets.[11]

Shortly thereafter, the French scholar Dominic approached the same pope for permission to found universities that would train theological minds and produce great teachers who could probe the mysteries of God. For Dominic, theology was loving God with the mind.

Francis's and Dominic's legitimate spiritualities belong together. Without good theology, Francis's type of ministry will move from piety to mere moralism. Without love-in-action, Dominic's scholarship will become arid scholasticism. Jesus put them together with the two-part great commandment to love God and love neighbor. A sustainable spirituality in the city must include both.

George Blaurock in Zurich (Sixteenth Century)

The Anabaptist Blaurock was to be banished from Zurich by the city council, but he stood before the council and thundered Psalm 24:1, saying "The earth is the LORD's."[12] Surely "the earth" includes Zurich.

No person or group owns the city. I love this "theology of place." The whole earth is the Lord's, including what the world has deemed "throw-away" urban neighborhoods.

Reforming Churches and Society (Sixteenth Century)

There were at least five models of reform in the sixteenth century:[13]

1. Savanoarola of Florence said that evangelism was the way to reform the church and society. The assumption was that reformed people would generate reform in society and the church.

2. Erasmus suggested that the education of the clergy would create reform. There were too many biblically ignorant clergy. The assumption was that right knowledge would lead to behavioral reform.

3. The Conciliarists, such as Gerson and D'Ailly, argued that better organizational structures and management could reform the church. The assumption was that there was concentration of depravity in the papacy or other groups who misappropriated power. Better management could spread the depravity out, so to speak, and ameliorate the influence of sinful leaders in the church.

4. Henry VIII of England and Cardinal Jimenez of Spain asked the governments to reform their churches. Legislation in 1534 produced the new Church of England, and the Inquisition "purified" the church in Spain. The assumption here was that the church required government assistance for effective reform.

5. The Anabaptists said the solution was an alternative church. The assumption was that the church as it existed was incapable of reform.

Luther and Calvin used all five strategies, which has led me to conclude that there is no one way to renew the church or society today. Our large cities require all five strategies.

Bartholomew Las Casas (Sixteenth Century)

Bartholomew left Spain for mission work in Cuba and Peru. He assumed that the indigenous people were his equals, and he baptized and ordained them for ministry![14] Meanwhile, back in Spain in front of King Charles V and Philip II, the scholar Sepulveda argued (like Aristotle) that some people were natural-born slaves. He promoted subjugation of the Indians. The argument raged on for more than half a century, but eventually the more economical system of subjugation was adopted.

Liberation theology in our own day constitutes a genuine revolt, not against biblical truth, but against the Aristotelian structures imposed on subject peoples for hundreds of years.

Roger Williams (Seventeenth Century)

Roger Williams of Providence moved to Rhode Island to protest Puritan exegesis which viewed Indians as Canaanites and Amalekites in the new Israel, Massachusetts. Williams was also exceptional in that he learned the native languages of the area. At a time when the failure to respect indigenous peoples is a major international concern, Williams provides a solid model. He also was the founder of my denomination, the American Baptist Church, in 1639.[15]

George Liele and David George (Eighteenth Century)

George Liele and David George were two eighteenth-century African-Americans, former slaves from Silver Creek and Savannah, Georgia, who were sent by their churches to the West Indies and then to Canada.[16] David George eventually planted Baptist churches in West Africa. They are the first known foreign missionaries sent from the United States, nearly two decades before the Judsons left for India and Burma. It is very important for Americans of any color to remember that the black church has always been about mission.

Charles Simeon (Nineteenth Century)

Charles Simeon of Cambridge died in 1836, but after reading H. C. G. Moule's biography of him in 1961, I had a completely new vision of what a city pastor could be.[17]

Simeon preached to the poor for fifty-four years. He also wrote books, mentored clergy, commissioned chaplains for Australian-bound prison ships, and challenged his assistants like Henry Martyn to work for missions. He met with Pitt, Wilberforce, Moore, Venn and Chapham until his death to banish slavery by law. Slavery ended first in the United Kingdom in 1807, then in the empire in 1837.

At the age of twenty-three, Simeon began his ministry after three years of theology study. I read his biography when I was twenty-three and adopted him as my pastoral model. The book sent me to Chicago and seminary. It provided the urban vision that integrated the scholarly and practical with the pastoral and public aspects of ministry.

Mott and Moody (Nineteenth Century)
The YMCA movement tied John R. Mott and evangelist D. L. Moody into a long partnership with student and ecumenical missions.[18] Mott planted YMCAs in every major city that could be reached by train in the nineteenth and early twentieth centuries. I have led many consultations in those same cities a century later and have spent many hours thinking about how these two men and their supporters were so single-minded in their solution to the challenge of cities. I admire them a great deal.

Lord Shaftesbury (Nineteenth Century)
Earl Anthony Cooper (1801–1885), known as Lord Shaftesbury, was an emotional basket case most of his life, yet he changed the physical, social and, consequently, spiritual structures of cities. He brought cemetery reform, potable water, common schools, the first mental hospital, wonderful sewer systems, the ten hour work day, and the widened mine shaft (which meant men rather than children would work in the coal mines).

For me, Shaftesbury and Charles Spurgeon are two sides of the urban unity coin in nineteenth-century London—one in Parliament and the other in the Metropolitan Tabernacle pulpit where he could preach to five thousand people weekly. I think Spurgeon's congregation was kept alive, healthy and able to read largely because of Shaftesbury.[19]

Jane Addams (Nineteenth Century)

Jane Addams and her friend Julia Lathrop moved into the slums of Chicago with inherited funds on September 21, 1889. Two weeks later Addams had an encounter with a burglar, for whom she promptly found a job. She created a garbage company to employ local people. Then, having majored in Greek in seminary, she founded the first Greek theater in the United States.[20] She reminds me that God can use any gifts and specializations for city ministry.

Jane Addams arrived naive and unfamiliar with the city. But she stayed, and she learned. She founded Hull House and became the patron saint for social work and settlement house ministries in cities all over the United States.

Negatively, she also reminds me one can be very good with some ethnic groups and prejudiced against others (she was very pro-European ethnic but failed completely to understand urban blacks).

Walter Rauschenbusch (Nineteenth and Twentieth Centuries)

Walter Rauschenbusch was forced by his life work in Hell's Kitchen, New York, to rethink his biblical theology. He has been characterized as the "social gospel founder" and was so heavily criticized by many of my earliest teachers that I never took him seriously. Then I read him in his original context, and I found his biblical work both orthodox and spiritually and socially relevant. I also found an unexpected missions concern.[21]

He reminds me to be careful not to reject with a "philosophy of the first glance" people whose ministry is different from my own.

Dorothy Day (Twentieth Century)

Dorothy Day started the Catholic worker movement as a result of her journey with the working poor during the labor movement in New York and Chicago. She grew up Episcopal but saw communists doing more to organize and empower the poor. After a lonely time as a single mother, she committed her life to Christ at a Catholic church, where she was introduced to the progressive Catholic thinking about God's concern for the laboring classes.

I think of her today because the fastest growing group of new poor includes the poorly educated and the victims of economic shifts due to a global economy. The church may be doing much better in its advocacy and development programs among the poorest of the poor than among those who are slipping through the urban cracks in Western European and North American cities.[22]

My photo album also includes Mother Teresa and a host of wonderful twentieth-century colleagues from whom I draw inspiration and information. These are the practicing theologians who are reinventing the church in large cities everywhere.

In recent years I've been adding the women whose incredible contributions were so long ignored by me and others. I've also been looking more closely at the contributions of Orthodox, Catholics, charismatics and others who have generally been off the map for those in conservative circles. This magnificent host of urban mentors has greatly expanded my understanding and appreciation for city ministry.

History as Magnificent Ruins

One of the disappointing realities of history is that yesterday's great ministries are today's ruins. Those that still live after decades or centuries may be a hollow shell of the original vision. To meet them is like meeting one's aging parents. You wish people might have seen them in their prime.

Emil Brunner, in his two-volume theology of sin, grace and salvation, suggested an illustration that helped me think about this fact. If we stand in downtown Athens and look up to the Acropolis to see the Parthenon as the sun sets behind it, we might think, or even say out loud, "What a magnificent ruin."[23]

Brunner applied that phrase to the sin-scarred human race. It's a ruin, of course, because the ravages of time have taken their toll;

but it's magnificent because there have been ministries of such splendor and significance. Your eye can fill in the space to see what it used to be or could yet become if renewal is a possibility. So, rather than react only to what I see now—the remains—I do my best to remember and critique ministry models in the context of their own time.

I didn't know Bernard Ramm very well, though I followed two decades after him in the ministry of Dunlap Baptist Church in Seattle. When we left in 1965, the church gave us an old pulpit chair. Corean and I repaired it, and we've used it in our living room for over thirty years. This chair has been a physical reminder of Ramm for me—and a reminder that in 1963 his book *The Witness* led me to discover that I am a historical charismatic after all.

26
REFLECTIONS

But the Counselor, the Holy Spirit,
whom the Father will send in my name,
will teach you all things and will remind you
of everything I have said to you.
John 14:26

IN EDWARD GIBBON'S *Decline and Fall of the Roman Empire,* Gibbon notes that "the profane of every age have divided the furious contests which the difference of a single diphthong excited."[1] He was referring, of course, to the Christological debates, from A.D. 325 to 451, between the *homoousios* and *homoiousios* parties, the former insisting that Jesus was the same as God, the latter that Jesus was similar to God. Frankly I have enormous respect for scholars who do that kind of theological work. The burden of my own work, however, has been to apply such theologizing in the turbulent urban context of local church ministry.[2]

John Wesley constructed his own working theology around four poles: Bible, tradition, reason and experience. He was a great man, but is his eighteenth-century outlook relevant to my theology? After working with his paradigm for a while, I concluded that my own theological reflections work with four poles also, with experience as the integrator (see figure 3).[3]

While Wesley treated experience as a separate entity, I see experience as the common fabric that mediates these four foundations. And I felt my model needed to include *context* (which includes my city), to emphasize that God has purposely put me in a community situation that cannot be ignored.

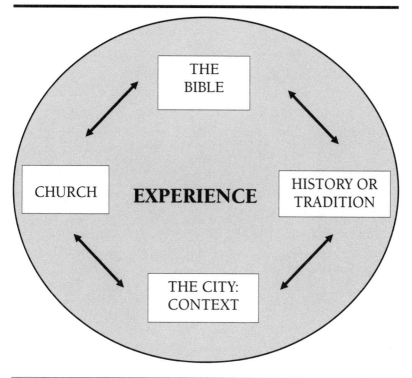

Figure 3. My Theological Map

As an evangelical, I acknowledge a personal experience of Jesus Christ. As an ordained minister, I've served formerly as a pastor and now as a professor and mission director. Throughout this entire book, I suspect you've detected the impact my city has had on my theology! All these social, ecclesial and personal experiences provide lenses through which I come to the Scripture. Every issue I face in the task of "doing theology" gets put through this grid. Ultimately I acknowledge Scripture to be the final test, the Supreme Court review on my values and lifestyle.

Under the frenetic pressures of urban ministry, I've struggled to keep some very basic themes in balance. Perhaps you've been aware of these ten tensions as you have read this book. These are some of the key tensions that I see coming out of the pages of Scripture.

1. *Creation and redemption.* We work to balance the Celtic creation theology with Augustine's salvation by grace and the faith of the Reformers. Ecologists and evangelists need not be enemies if we find a way to affirm both. When we were creating the organization I now direct, International Urban Associates, we included in the value statement: "We . . . commit IUA to an ecological theology that is both *creative* and *redemptive* for persons and places. And so we seek both the *spiritual* transformation of persons and the *social* transformation of places until our Lord comes or calls for us."

2. *Truth and love.* We work to balance the prophetic and judgmental with grace and forgiveness. With sadness I acknowledge that these two truths have come unglued in our time. God's people need to hear the truth that the angry urban prophet Amos delivered. They also need the pastoral message of weeping Jeremiah. As I've tried to show, Paul and Barnabas need each other on the urban mission team.

3. *Individuality and community.* We work to value the biblical contributions of both Greeks and Hebrews (or Catholics and Protestants) at a time when rampant individualism threatens the West and an exaggerated view of cultural rights sustains oppression in much of Asia.[4]

4. *Local and global.* We work to balance the Incarnation of Jesus Christ, which affirms every local culture and community, with the universal message of salvation for every person, tribe and nation. This requires me to acknowledge that while God is completely concerned about my own community, most of my sisters and brothers in Christ are nonwhite and non-Western, and God is equally concerned for them.[5]

5. *Unity and diversity.* We work to affirm the local, distinctive and new diverse gifts of this generation in worship and service, while holding on to the historic unity and continuity of the church. Pastoring in the city is an art that requires helping congregations define their identity and security in the church universal, while creating a climate for diverse worship and ministry styles that can

bridge generations, classes and cultural backgrounds.

6. *Power and powerlessness.* We work to keep in balance two realities of Jesus' ministry—the voluntary setting aside of privilege and society's trappings while at the same time engaging in resource acquisition for the sake of advocacy and justice on behalf of the most vulnerable in society. The struggle here is to follow the humble Jesus while appropriating the Holy Spirit's power.

7. *Certainty and mystery.* We acknowledge that the reign of rationalism has ended, as the New Age prophets tell us, but that's only part of the truth. At this time, when the boundaries of reason and mystery are unclear or shifting, we seek the Holy Spirit's help to keep our core of basic theology connected to the historic orthodoxy of the church.

8. *Commission and commandment.* We take seriously both the great commandment, to love God and our neighbors in service, and the great commission, which requires that we deliberately enlarge our geographical and social maps for gospel witness.

9. *Past and future.* We acknowledge the continuity between where the church has been and where it needs to go; we encourage the creation of new churches while honoring and working for the renewal of historic churches.

10. *Work and rest.* We work to sustain in our ministry the rhythm God has built into life. God worked, then rested. Jesus preached and healed, then retreated. I also must rest. (And it's okay, for I have learned something in the city over thirty-five years: I am not the Messiah!)

The burden of my life has been to find a sustainable spirituality for urban ministry. Some twenty years ago, two young gay men in my congregation brought me up short with an accusation. "You're not a very good pastor for us," they said. "We resent the fact that you seem to have better relationships with dead people than with some of us who live."

Was it true? Was history my escape? Was I really spending time with Luther and Edwards that should be given to them? I took them seriously, and with the blessing of my deacon board, I let these two men be my guide into the gay world of Chicago, including the shadowy world of the transvestite theater. I learned a lot from their books and their visits. Our church responded with new sensitivity and ministry. I became much more sensitive to a large group of needy neighbors.

But I have also learned how manipulative and tyrannical contemporary relationships can become if left unchecked by the larger "community of the saints," the "great cloud of witnesses" before whom I run this race. If I don't balance these tensions, I'll burn out.

So while the city pushes new agendas and issues onto my plate as a citizen and a pastor, my tradition becomes a natural brake that forces me to take time to confront the issues through biblical search and personal experience. What makes me a "conservative" is that I am committed to allow Scripture as I understand it to have the final say in the matter. And if I do not know enough about either the Scripture texts or the current issue confronting me, I pray for the grace to live with unresolved tension while I bother my brothers and sisters who can give me guidance on the issue—my family, my support group, the ministry network and others—and find more clarity. I would die for my convictions, but not for the opinions I have on many issues confronting city churches today.

Finally, I would like to conclude this book in the same way I like to conclude a worship service—with a hymn of worship. Will you sing a hymn with me before we go out into our cities in ministry for our Lord? Worship always precedes service.[6]

Our Cities Cry to You, O God
Our cities cry to you, O God, from out their pain and strife;
You made us for yourself alone, but we choose alien life.
Our goals are pleasure, gold and power; injustice stalks our earth;
In vain we seek for rest, for joy, for sense of human worth.

Yet still You walk our streets, O Christ! We know your presence here

Where humble Christians love and serve in godly grace and fear.
O Word made flesh be seen in us! May all we say and do
Affirm You God, Incarnate still, and turn men's hearts to you.

Your people are your hands and feet to serve your world today,
Our lives the book our cities read to help them find your way.
O pour your sov'reign Spirit out on heart and will and brain;
Inspire your Church with love and pow'r to ease our cities' pain!

O healing Savior, Prince of Peace, salvation's Source and Sum,
For you our broken cities cry—O come, Lord Jesus, come!
With truth your royal diadem, with righteousness your rod,
O come, Lord Jesus, bring to earth the City of our God! [7]

E. Margaret Clarkson

Please accept now my benediction:
   To God be the glory
   and to the earth be peace
   To the church be courage
   and to our cities be hope!

Notes

Chapter 1: A Journey to the City

[1]My childhood neighbor Marie Hamel Royer has published a beautifully illustrated 340-page book, *The Saxon Story: Early Pioneers on the South Fork* (Bellingham, Wash.: Whatcom County Historical Society, 1982), describing the people and places of the area.

[2]Martin Luther King, *Stride Toward Freedom* (New York: Harper, 1958).

[3]In an earlier book, *The Urban Christian* (Downers Grove, Ill.: InterVarsity Press, 1986), I go into more depth about Simeon and his impact on my worldview.

[4]Harvey Cox, *The Secular City* (New York: Macmillan, 1965). Cox saw the city as both freeway and switchboard. He celebrated these metaphors as gifts to the urban community; I saw them as dividing and alienating.

[5]Stephen Rose, "Why Evangelicals Can't Survive in the City," *Community Renewal Society Journal* (January 1966).

[6]Perry Miller, *Roger Williams: His Contribution to the American Tradition* (New York: Atheneum, 1962). Miller describes his awakening and involvement with the Puritan materials in the preface of his work *Errand into the Wilderness* (New York: Harper, 1964). Clearly he is indebted to Frederick Jackson Turner's "Frontier Thesis" of American history, but he repudiates the excesses of it. My own Baptist denomination and I argue that Williams was working with the implications of a congregational church, while attempting to implement an oft-forgotten mandate: to demonstrate the social aspects of his faith in his work with the Indians. After reading *The Complete Writings of Roger Williams* (New York: Russell & Russell, 1963), I was more impressed than ever with the validity of exposing his ideas to the modern scene.

In his stimulating Christological critique of American theologies, including covenant theology, revivalism, social gospel and Barthianism, Jean Russell says, "As early as 1640, Roger Williams concerned himself with property rights of American Indians and their inclusion into the Church" (*God's Lost Cause: A Study of the Church and the Racial Problem* [Valley Forge, Penn.: Judson, 1969], p. 10). Williams was no "Indian lover," but he had an unusual willingness to live among them, learn their language and welcome them as humans. In fact he produced an entire work, *Key into the Language of America* (1643), dedicated to Indian language and lore.

[7]Some of John Fry's witty sermons appeared in *Fire and Blackstone* (New York: Lippincott, 1969).

[8]Henry M. Stanley, *In Darkest Africa: The Way In* (New York: Scribner, 1890), and

William Booth, *In Darkest England: The Way Out* (New York: Salvation Army, 1890). Fortunately the Salvation Army has republished this classic in an anniversary edition: *In Darkest England & the Way Out* (Atlanta, Ga.: Salvation Army Supplies, Southern, 1984).

[9]Jonathan Kozol, *Amazing Grace: The Lives of Children and the Conscience of a Nation* (New York: Crown, 1995).

[10]Henry Cadbury, *The Peril of Modernizing Jesus* (London: Macmillan, 1937).

Chapter 2: God's Hands Are in the Mud

[1]William Temple, *Christianity and the Social Order* (New York: Penguin, 1942).

[2]H. W. Robinson, "The Hebrew Conception of Corporate Personality," in *Corporate Personality in Ancient Israel* (Philadelphia: Fortress, 1964). This essay was formative for me, and it led to many other sources on the concept of "corporate" in Israel.

[3]David Bosch, *Transforming Mission* (Maryknoll, N.Y.: Orbis, 1991).

[4]Augustine, "The Trinity," in the Fathers of the Church series, vol. 45 (Washington, D.C.: Catholic University, 1963).

Chapter 3: Can We Save a City like Sodom?

[1]H. H. Rowley, *The Faith of Israel* (Philadelphia: Westminster, 1957).

[2]I'm very supportive of prayer walks, prayer houses and Concerts of Prayer movements in urban contexts. John Dawson, Ed Silvoso and David Bryant have been used by God mightily in our day to remind the church to pray for and pray in the cities. My concern is that this should never be seen as a sufficient strategy for urban concern or involvement. An exclusively spiritual concern for cities can come close to a neognosticism that denies much of the theology this book is about.

Chapter 4: A Surprising Source of Urban Leaders

[1]James MacGregor Burns, *Leadership* (New York: Harper & Row, 1978); Robert K. Greenleaf, *Servant Leadership: A Journey into the Nature of Legitimate Power and Greatness* (New York: Paulist, 1977).

[2]William Edwin Sangster, *Why Jesus Never Wrote a Book* (London: Epworth, 1952).

[3]Eldridge Cleaver, *Soul on Ice* (New York: Dell, 1968), and Claude Brown, *Manchild in the Promised Land* (New York: New American Library, 1965).

[4]William A. Gamson, *Power and Discontent* (Homewood, Ill.: Dorsey Press, 1968).

[5]Edward C. Banfield, *The Unheavenly City Revisited* (Boston: Little, Brown, 1974).

[6]Henri J. M. Nouwen, *The Living Reminder: Service and Prayer in Memory of Jesus Christ* (New York: Seabury, 1977).

Chapter 5: Hope in the City

[1]Jonathan Kozol, *Amazing Grace: The Lives of Children and the Conscience of a Nation* (New York: Crown, 1995).

[2]Two superb commentaries to which I am greatly indebted (among numerous others) are those of my McCormick Seminary colleagues the late Robert Boling,

Judges (New York: Doubleday, 1969), and Edward F. Campbell, *Ruth* (New York: Doubleday, 1975), both in the Anchor Bible series. Also I want to express my debt to Ronald Hals for *The Theology of the Book of Ruth* (Philadelphia: Fortress, 1969).

Chapter 6: The Individual & the Community

[1]H. W. Robinson, "The Hebrew Conception of Corporate Personality," in *Corporate Personality in Ancient Israel* (Philadelphia: Fortress, 1964). See also Robinson's "The Group and the Individual in Israel" in the same publication.

[2]Otto J. Baab, *The Theology of the Old Testament* (New York: Abingdon, 1949), p. 56. See also Louis Berkhof, *Systematic Theology* (Grand Rapids, Mich.: Eerdmans, 1941), pp. 237-43, for a discussion relating to imputation. Other biblical theologians have seen the phenomena in wider contexts also, in the Psalms, for example: C. A. Briggs, *A Critical and Exegetical Commentary on the Book of Psalms,* ICC, vol. 1 (Edinburgh: T & T Clark, 1906); R. H. Pfeiffer, *Introduction to the Old Testament* (New York: Harper & Bros., 1941).

[3]Ludwig Kohler, *Old Testament Theology,* trans. A. S. Todd (Philadelphia: Westminster, 1957). "Let all this act as a brief indication of the fact that in the O.T. it is taken for granted that man lives in a community, comprehensive to a degree we can scarcely imagine" (p. 161). See also his summary on pp. 165-66. I get the impression that in this more extreme view Adam and Eve weren't significant to the degree that a tribe was in subsequent history. Kohler is trying to salvage a social consciousness.

[4]H. H. Rowley, *The Faith of Israel* (Philadelphia: Westminster, 1957). See chapter 4, "Individual and Community," pp. 99-123. Enoch, Abraham and David are individuals, representative of the many who occur throughout Israel's history. Achan may be cited as one for whom the whole family had to be destroyed to "rid the community of the taint upon it" (p. 100). He likewise reminds us that the sacrifices were never social but were for the individual (p. 102). His notes on the remnant in this connection are very instructive (pp. 117-23).

[5]William Henry Green, "Primeval Chronology," *Bibliotheca Sacra* (April 1890): 285-303. This scholarship is old but unique.

[6]S. A. Cook, *The Cambridge Ancient History* (Cambridge: The University Press, 1925), vol. 2, p. 438. See also Malachi 1:3-4; Isaiah 41:8; Genesis 9:18; 10:15-20.

[7]Rowley, *The Faith of Israel,* p. 113.

[8]G. A. F. Knight, *From Moses to Paul* (London: Lutterworth Press, 1949), pp. 37-38. See also J. Pedersen, *Israel: Its Life and Culture,* trans. A. Moller (London: Oxford University Press, 1926), vols. 1-2, p. 254. See also M. Burrows, "Levirate Marriage in Israel," *Journal of Biblical Literature* 59 (1940): 31. See also Isaiah 66:22; Numbers 27:11; Genesis 12:2; 1 Kings 1:47.

[9]W. F. Lofthouse, "Hebrew Religion from Moses to Saul," in *The People and the Book,* ed. A. S. Peacke (Oxford: Oxford University Press, 1925), p. 237. Moses sees burdens his brothers bear, for any Hebrew is a brother (Ex 2:11; Heb 11:24-26).

[10]Joshua 7. Russell Philip Shedd concludes: "The ancient Hebrew conception of solidarity held unity in higher esteem than its more modern sociological coun-

terparts. This unity did not result from external imposition, but was fundamentally grounded in the psychological conditioning of the Israelites in the Old Testament period" (*Man in Community* [Grand Rapids, Mich.: Eerdmans, 1964], p. 41).

[11]Knight, *From Moses to Paul*, p. 32: "To apply the term 'organism' to Israel here is particularly appropriate. The nation as a whole on occasions acts as an individual that can speak in the first person singular, and yet at the same time in the first person plural (Num 21:22; 20:14, 17-18). The nation as such had a soul of its own, was a spiritual entity, was a psychical unity, and, while the persons within the nation were each separately going their own way, yet their ethos was one, and their relationship to God was one."

In *A Christian Theology of the Old Testament* Knight says the following regarding Jerusalem: "The Holy City at whose battlements they gazed in awe and love was not only the earthly city of Jerusalem. It was, in a real sense, the center of the universe. This was because it was a city with significance, a significance which could be understood only in terms of the divine purpose for all mankind" (London: SCM Press, 1959), p. 309. See also John L. McKenzie, S. J., *Dictionary of the Bible* (Milwaukee: Bruce Publishing, 1965), pp. 138-40, for several paragraphs on the theological significance of Jerusalem.

[12]Lausanne Occasional Papers No. 3: "The Lausanne Covenant—An Exposition and Commentary" by John Stott (Minneapolis: World Wide Publications, 1975). Articles five and six follow:

5. CHRISTIAN SOCIAL RESPONSIBILITY: We affirm that God is both the Creator and the Judge of all men. We therefore should share his concern for justice and reconciliation throughout human society and for the liberation of men from every kind of oppression. Because mankind is made in the image of God, every person, regardless of race, religion, color, culture, class, sex or age, has an intrinsic dignity because of which he should be respected and served, not exploited. Here too we express penitence both for our neglect and for having sometimes regarded evangelism and social concern as mutually exclusive. Although reconciliation with man is not reconciliation with God, nor is social action evangelism, nor is political liberation salvation, nevertheless, we affirm that evangelism and socio-political involvement are both part of our Christian duty. For both are necessary expressions of our doctrines of God and man, our love for our neighbor and our obedience to Jesus Christ. The message of salvation implies also a message of judgment upon every form of alienation, oppression and discrimination, and we should not be afraid to denounce evil and injustice wherever they exist. When people receive Christ they are born again into his kingdom and must seek not only to exhibit but also to spread its righteousness in the midst of an unrighteous world. The salvation we claim should be transforming us in the totality of our personal and social responsibilities. Faith without works is dead.

6. THE CHURCH AND EVANGELISM: We affirm that Christ sends his redeemed people into the world as the Father sent him, and that this calls for a similar deep and costly penetration of the world. We need to break out of our

ecclesiastical ghettos and permeate non-Christian society. In the church's mission of sacrificial service evangelism is primary. World evangelization requires the whole church to take the whole Gospel to the whole world. The church is at the very center of God's cosmic purpose and is his appointed means of spreading the Gospel. But a church which preaches the Cross must itself be marked by the Cross. It becomes a stumbling block to evangelism when it betrays the Gospel or lacks a living faith in God, a genuine love for people, or scrupulous honesty in all things including promotion and finance. The church is the community of God's people rather than an institution, and must not be identified with any particular culture, social or political system, or human ideology.

Chapter 7: Zion Songs & Urban Poets

[1] Alexander Maclaren, *Expositions of Holy Scripture* (New York: Armstrong, 1907-10).

[2] Claus Westerman, *Praise and Lament in the Psalms* (Atlanta, Ga.: John Knox, 1981).

[3] Robert Gordis, *Koheleth, the Man and His World: A Study of Ecclesiastes* (New York: Schocken Books, 1968).

[4] Ibid., p. 22.

[5] Cited in Franklin H. Littel, *The Origins of Sectarian Protestantism* (New York: Macmillan, 1952), p. 121. Regarding the Anabaptists, see Guy F. Hershberger, ed., *The Recovery of the Anabaptist Vision* (Scottsdale, Penn.: Herald Press, 1957); George Huntston Williams, *The Radical Reformation* (Philadelphia: Westminster, 1962); Donald Durnbaugh, *The Believers' Church* (New York: Macmillan, 1968); George Huntston Williams, ed., *Spiritual and Anabaptist Writers* (Philadelphia: Westminster, 1957).

[6] Alexander Callow, "The City in Colonial America," chapter 3 in *American Urban History*, 3rd ed. (New York: Oxford University Press, 1982), pp. 37-64.

[7] Leroy Waterman, *The Song of Songs, Translated and Interpreted as a Dramatic Poem* (Ann Arbor: University of Michigan Press, 1948).

Chapter 8: What Cities Ought to Look Like

[1] David Bosch, *Transforming Mission* (Maryknoll, N.Y.: Orbis, 1991).

[2] Henry M. Stanley, *In Darkest Africa: The Way In* (New York: Scribner, 1890).

[3] William Booth, *In Darkest England: The Way Out* (New York: Salvation Army, 1890).

[4] John Dawson, *Taking Our Cities for God: How to Break Spiritual Strongholds* (Lake Mary, Fla.: Creation House, 1989).

Chapter 9: Jeremiah's Letter to Urban Families

[1] George Webber, *God's Colony in Man's World* (New York: Abingdon, 1960).

[2] I have written about this extensively in my previous book, *The Urban Christian* (Downers Grove, Ill.: InterVarsity Press, 1987).

Chapter 11: Major Themes in Minor Prophets

[1] F. S. Webster, *Patriot & Revivalist* (London: Morgan & Scott, 1906).

[2] Clarence Macartney, *Strange Texts: Grand Truths* (Grand Rapids, Mich.: Kregel, 1994).

[3] Webster, *Patriot & Revivalist*, p. 16.

[4] William McLoughlin, *Revivals, Awakenings and Reform* (Chicago: University of Chicago Press, 1978).

[5] Timothy Smith, *Revivalism and Social Reform* (Baltimore, Md.: Johns Hopkins University Press, 1980).

[6] Norris Magnuson, *Salvation in the Slums* (Metuchen, N.J.: Scarecrow Press, 1977).

Chapter 12: When All Else Fails, Send the Choir

[1] Henry Steele Commager and Allan Nevins, *America: The Story of a Free People* (Oxford: Oxford University Press, 1966), preface.

Chapter 14: Models from the Migrant Streams

[1] George F. Moore, *Judaism in the First Centuries of the Christian Era, the Age of the Tannaim* (Cambridge, Mass.: Harvard University Press, 1927-30).

[2] Michael Green, *Evangelism in the Early Church* (London: Hodder & Stoughton, 1970).

[3] Louis Finkelstein, *The Pharisees: The Sociological Background of Their Faith*, 2nd ed. (Philadelphia: Jewish Publication Society of America, 1940).

[4] Erwin R. Goodenough, "Philo of Alexandria," in *Great Jewish Personalities in Ancient and Medieval Times*, ed. Simon Noveck (New York: B'nai B'rith & Farrar, Straus & Cudahy, 1959).

[5] Frederick Norwood, *Strangers and Exiles: A History of Religious Refugees* (Nashville: Abingdon, 1976).

[6] Williston Walker, *A History of the Christian Church*, rev. Wilhelm Pauk (New York: Scribner, 1959).

[7] Kenneth Scott Latourette, *The First Five Centuries* (New York: Harper, 1970).

[8] Harry Ironside, *The 400 Silent Years: From Malachi to Matthew* (New York: Loizeaux Brothers, 1914).

Chapter 15: Skeletons in the Closet

[1] Beyond the standard commentaries on the infancy narratives of Matthew and Luke, the scholar I'm most indebted to for his work on these texts is Raymond Brown, *The Birth of the Messiah* (New York: Doubleday, 1977).

[2] The comparative work on the genealogies was rather exhaustively done by William Henry Green in *Bibliotheca Sacra* (April 1890): 285-303.

[3] I have hundreds of very old commentaries that treat these texts exegetically but advise against even reading them publicly for the scandal it would cause. H. C. Leupold says in his homiletical suggestions in *Exposition of Genesis* (Grand Rapids, Mich.: Baker, 1942): "Entirely unsuited to homiletical use, much as the devout Bible student may glean from the chapter" (p. 990).

[4] Brown, *Birth of the Messiah*, p. 72.

[5]Stephen Neill, *The Interpretation of the New Testament 1861-1961* (New York: Oxford, 1966).

[6]Brown, *Birth of the Messiah,* pp. 73-74.

[7]Edwuard Schweizer, *The Good News According to Matthew* (Atlanta, Ga.: John Knox, 1975), pp. 31-45.

Chapter 16: Jesus & the City

[1]Edmund Wilson, *The Scroll from the Dead Sea* (London: W. H. Allen, 1955).

[2]John Allegro, *The Dead Sea Scrolls* (Harmondsworth, Middlesex: Penguin, 1958).

[3]Millar Burrows, *The Dead Sea Scrolls* (New York: Viking Press, 1955).

[4]Millar Burrows, *More Light on the Dead Sea Scrolls* (New York: Viking Press, 1958).

[5]Henry Cadbury, *The Peril of Modernizing Jesus* (London: Macmillan, 1937).

[6]Alfred Edersheim, *The Life and Times of Jesus the Messiah,* 2 vols. (Grand Rapids, Mich.: Eerdmans, 1959).

[7]Richard A. Batey, *Jesus and the Forgotten City: New Light on Sepphoris and the Urban World of Jesus* (Grand Rapids, Mich.: Baker, 1991).

[8]Paul L. Maier, in foreword to ibid., p. 9.

[9]N. G. L. Hammond, *Alexander the Great: King, Commander and Statesman* (Park Ridge, N.J.: Noyes, 1980).

[10]Iain Browning, *Jerash and the Decapolis* (London: Chatto & Windus, 1982).

[11]George F. Moore, *Judaism in the First Centuries of the Christian Era, the Age of the Tannim* (Cambridge, Mass.: Harvard University Press, 1927-30).

[12]George Eldon Ladd, *The Gospel of the Kingdom* (Grand Rapids, Mich.: Eerdmans, 1959).

[13]Raymond Brown, *Epistles of John* (Garden City, N.Y.: Doubleday, 1982).

[14]W. D. Davies, *The Gospel and the Land* (Berkeley: University of California Press, 1974).

[15]Russell Shedd, *Man in Community* (Grand Rapids, Mich.: Eerdmans, 1964).

[16]A. D. Nock, *Conversion* (Oxford: Oxford University Press, 1969).

[17]John Howard Yoder, *The Politics of Jesus* (Grand Rapids, Mich.: Eerdmans, 1972).

Chapter 17: The Church at the City Center

[1]Cain Hope Felder, *Troubling Biblical Waters: Race, Class and Family* (Maryknoll, N.Y.: Orbis Books, 1989).

[2]Martin Hengel, *Acts and the Earliest History of Christianity,* trans. John Bowden (Philadelphia: Fortress, 1979), p. 80.

[3]*The Geography of Strabo,* trans. Horace Leonard Jones (Cambridge, Mass.: Harvard University Press, 1917-32), 15.1.73.

[4]See also Sherman E. Johnson, *Paul the Apostle and His Cities* (Wilmington, Del.: M. Glazier, 1987); John E. Sambaugh and David L. Balch, *The New Testament in Its Social Environment* (Philadelphia: Westminster, 1986); Wayne Meeks and Robert L. Wilken, *Jews and Christians in Antioch in the First Four Centuries of the Common Era* (Missoula, Mont.: Scholars Press for the Society of Biblical Literature, 1978); Richard N. Longenecker, "Antioch of Syria," in *Major Cities of the Biblical World,* ed. R. K. Harrison (Nashville: Thomas Nelson, 1985).

[5]Josephus *Jewish Wars* 7.45. *The Complete Works of Flavius Josephus,* trans. William Whiston (Grand Rapids, Mich.: Kregel, 1960).

Chapter 18: When Truth & Love Collide

[1]Sir William Mitchell Ramsay, *Cities of Paul* (London: Hodder & Stoughton, 1907), and *St. Paul the Traveler and the Roman Citizen* (London: Hodder & Stoughton, 1895); Wayne A. Meeks, *The First Urban Christians: The Social World of the Apostle Paul* (New Haven, Conn.: Yale University Press, 1983).

[2]E. Stanley Jones, *The Reconstruction of the Church—On What Pattern?* (Nashville: Abingdon Press, 1970).

[3]There are many monographs on African Christianity and the schisms, but I advise introductory students to start with standard church histories to get the big picture of the whole series of controversies of which this was one. So see Williston Walker's essay "Forgiveness of Sins" in *A History of the Christian Church,* rev. Wilhelm Pauk (New York: Scribner, 1959), pp. 91-93. The stunning new book on African Christianity is Elizabeth Isichei's *A History of Christianity in Africa* (Grand Rapids, Mich.: Eerdmans, 1995).

[4]Regarding Papias, see J. B. Lightfoot and J. R. Harmon, eds. and trans., *The Apostolic Fathers: Greek Texts and English Translations of Their Writings,* 2nd ed., rev. (Grand Rapids, Mich.: Baker, 1992), pp. 556-95. The summary of Papias's discussion of Mark begins on p. 569, where the reader can also find the up-to-date bibliography on this "much debated passage."

[5]Regarding Mark in Alexandria, see the contemporary Egyptian A. S. Atiya, *A History of Eastern Christianity* (London: Methuen, 1968).

Chapter 19: With Paul on an Urban Journey

[1]Williston Walker, *A History of the Christian Church* (New York: Scribner's, 1918).

[2]Kenneth Scott Latourette, *The First Five Centuries* (New York: Harper, 1970).

[3]Martin Luther, "On the Councils and the Church, 1539," in *Selected Writing of Martin Luther,* ed. Theodore G. Tappert (Philadelphia: Fortress Press, 1967), pp. 197-370.

[4]Stephen Neill, *A History of Christian Missions* (Harmondsworth, Middlesex: Penguin, 1964), pp. 29-30. There Neill says, "It was Paul's custom to settle for a time in one of the great cities of the empire, and through his younger helpers to radiate out from that centre to the smaller cities of the region" (p. 29).

[5]E. M. Blaiklock, *Cities of the New Testament* (Westwood, N.J.: Revell, 1965).

[6]A. T. Robertson, *Epochs in the Life of Paul: A Study of Development in Paul's Career* (New York: Scribner's, 1956).

[7]Paul Little, *How to Give Away Your Faith* (Downers Grove, Ill.: InterVarsity Press, 1966).

Chapter 20: Two Letters, Two Urban Spiritualities

[1]Timothy Smith, *Revivalism and Social Reform* (Baltimore, Md.: Johns Hopkins University Press, 1980).

[2]Norris Magnuson, *Salvation in the Slums* (Metuchen, N.J.: Scarecrow Press, 1977).

[3]Ruth Tucker, *Guardians of the Great Commission: The Story of Women in Modern Missions* (Grand Rapids, Mich.: Zondervan, 1988).

[4]William Stead, *If Christ Came to Chicago* (Chicago: Laird & Lee, 1894).

Chapter 21: The Drama of New Testament Evangelism

[1]Ignatius, "The Letters of Ignatius, Bishop of Antioch," in *Early Christian Fathers,* vol. 1, ed. Cyril C. Richardson (Philadelphia: Westminster Press, 1953).

[2]A. T. Robertson, *Epochs in the Life of Paul: A Study of Development in Paul's Career* (New York: Scribner's, 1956); *The Jerome Biblical Commentary,* ed. Raymond E. Brown, Joseph A. Fitzmeyer and Roland E. Murphy (London: Geoffrey Chapman, 1968).

[3]See the C. F. Evans essay "The New Testament in the Making" in *Cambridge History of the Bible,* vol. 1, ed. P. R. Ackroyd and C. F. Evans (Cambridge: Cambridge University Press, 1970), pp. 232-84, especially p. 241 for Bishop Onesimus's inclusion of the Philemon letter. We also know that Marcion's false canon had a profound impact on the true collection of Pauline and other N.T. writings. See also Hans von Campenhausen, *The Formation of the Christian Bible* (Philadelphia: Fortress Press, 1972), pp. 147-209.

[4]Sometimes a cost that church folks find difficult to pay is simply to offer fellowship, membership or leadership to new believers who aren't like themselves. In 1967 I helped lead an entire street gang to Jesus, only to see my church put numerous barriers into their path to acceptance.

[5]"Birthplace to Churches of Many Nations," *IUA Newsletter* (Winter 1995) describes how Tokyo, Japan, has become an incubator of foreign-language churches.

Chapter 22: Ethnicity in the Church—Is It Still Okay to Be Jewish?

[1]Charles Shanabruch, *Chicago's Catholics: The Evolution of an American Identity* (Notre Dame, Ind.: University of Notre Dame Press, 1981).

[2]For starters, try Peter d'A. Jones and Melvin G. Holli, eds., *Ethnic Chicago* (Grand Rapids, Mich.: Eerdmans, 1981); Randall M. Miller and Thomas D. Marzik, *Immigrants and Religion in Urban America* (Philadelphia: Temple University Press, 1977); but especially Stephen Theronstrom, ed., *The Harvard Encyclopedia of American Ethnic Groups* (Cambridge, Mass.: Harvard Belnap Press, 1982).

[3]Here is the Nicene Creed:

We believe in one God,
the Father, the Almighty,
maker of heaven and earth,
of all that is, seen and unseen.

We believe in one Lord, Jesus Christ,
the only Son of God,
eternally begotten of the Father,
God from God, Light from Light,
true God from true God,
begotten, not made,

of one Being with the Father.
Through him all things were made.
    For us and for our salvation
he came down from heaven;
by the power of the Holy Spirit
    he became incarnate from the virgin Mary, and was made man.
    For our sake he was crucified under Pontius Pilate;
he suffered death and was buried.
On the third day he rose again
    in accordance with the Scriptures;
he ascended into heaven
    and is seated at the right hand of the Father.
    He will come again in glory to judge the living and the dead,
and his kingdom will have no end.
    We believe in the Holy Spirit, the Lord, the giver of life,
who proceeds from the Father and the Son.
With the Father and the Son he is worshiped and glorified.
He has spoken through the prophets.
We believe in one holy catholic and apostolic Church.
We acknowledge one Baptism for the forgiveness of sins.
We look for the resurrection of the dead,
    and the life of the world to come. Amen.

(*Lutheran Book of Worship,* ed. The Inter-Lutheran Commission on Worship [Minneapolis, Minn.: Augsburg, 1978], p. 64. Used by permission.)

[4]See "Researching Your Own Roots," in *The Word in Life Study Bible* (Nashville: Nelson, 1996), pp. 2245-46.

[5]Elias Chacour, *Blood Brothers* (Grand Rapids, Mich.: Zondervan, 1984).

Chapter 23: The Empire Strikes Back

[1]David Bosch, *Transforming Mission* (Maryknoll, N.Y.: Orbis, 1991), p. 146.

[2]Oscar Cullmann, *Christ and Time* (Philadelphia: Westminster, 1964) and *The State in the New Testament* (New York: Scribner, 1956).

[3]S. R. F. Price, *Rituals and Power: The Roman Imperial Cult in Asia Minor* (Cambridge: Cambridge University Press, 1984), p. 132.

[4]Colin J. Hemer, *The Letters to the Seven Churches of Asia in Their Local Setting* (Sheffield, U.K.: Journal for the Study of the New Testament. Supplement series, book 11, 1986).

[5]Robert Henry Charles, *A Critical and Exegetical Commentary on the Revelation of St. John* (New York, Scribner's, 1920).

Chapter 24: So Long, Babylon, I'll Miss You

[1]Augustine, *The City of God,* ed. Vernon J. Bourke (Garden City, N.Y.: Image Books, 1958).

[2]See Walter Rauschenbusch, *The Righteousness of the Kingdom,* ed. Max L. Stackhouse (Nashville: Abingdon, 1968), and Reinhold Niebuhr, *Moral Man and*

Immoral Society (New York: Scribner's, 1932).

[3]Jacques Ellul, *The Meaning of the City*, trans. Dennis Pardee (Grand Rapids, Mich.: Eerdmans, 1970).

[4]Harvey Cox, *The Secular City* (New York: Macmillan, 1965).

Chapter 25: The Urban Family Album

[1]Bernard Ramm, *The Witness of the Spirit* (Grand Rapids, Mich.: Eerdmans, 1960).

[2]"Letter to Diognetus," ed. and trans. Eugene R. Fairweather in *The Library of Christian Classics: Early Christian Fathers*, vol. 1, ed. Cyril C. Richardson, chaps. 5—6, pp. 216-18.

[3]My first visit with Bishop Samuel was in March 1976.

[4]E. A. Judge, *The Social Patterns of Christian Groups in the First Century* (London: Tyndale, 1960), and Lewis Mumford, *The City in History: Its Origins, Its Transformations, Its Prospects* (New York: Harcourt Brace & World, 1961). Mumford documented the decline of humanitarianism in the Greek and Roman cities respectively. He notes that from the "fourth century B.C. onward, buildings began to replace man" (pp. 170-71). "The Roman Empire," he suggests, "was a product of a single expanding urban power center . . . itself a vast city-building enterprise" (p. 205). A very clear picture of debasement and iniquity emerges from relatively contemporary archaeological studies of Rome itself. Mumford includes extended quotations from Lanciani, currently investigating the culture of the early Christian centuries. Consider, for example, the following account:

> To conceive the idea of a Roman carnarium, an assemblage of pits into which men and beasts, bodies and carcasses and any kind of unmentionable refuse, were thrown in disorder. Imagine what must have been the conditions of these dreadful districts in times of plagues, when the pits (*puticoli*) were kept open by night and day . . . filled with corpses, thrown in until the level of the adjacent streets was reached. (p. 217)

It is clear to historians that as Rome grew and its system of exploitation expanded, the rot prevailed endemically among the masses who lived in "cramped, noisy, airless, foul-smelling, infected quarters, paying extortionate rents to merciless landlords, undergoing daily indignities that brutalized them and in turn demanded compensatory outlets" (p. 221). All this in Rome, the largest and best-governed city in fifteen centuries, with a population in the early Christian centuries of between 800,000 and 1,200,000, most of whom lived in four- and five-story tenements, lacking in public sanitation, yet having access to police and fire protection for the most part. Mumford continues:

> Though the Romans inflated the theological currency by inventing a special god for every occasion in life, the one supreme god that they really worshiped was the body . . . the public bath was its temple. (p. 226)

What amazes Mumford and appears significant in this discussion is this brief comment, wherein the sociologist asserts:

> What is more, the Christian inheritors of Rome, despite their soaring memories of the arena and their grievous retreat in the catacombs, chose Rome as the cornerstone on which to build a new urban civilization. (p. 238)

Into these urban centers went the Jew of the Diaspora. "They were," says Philip Schaff, "as ubiquitous in the Roman Empire as they are now throughout Christendom" (Philip Schaff, *History of the Christian Church,* vol. 1 [Grand Rapids, Mich.: Eerdmans, 1950], p. 86). In a study called "The Jewish Commonwealths and the Dispersions," which is not primarily a religious apologetic, Salo Baron makes the following observations with respect to the emergence of the synagogue in the urban context: "The role of the synagogue is one of the most momentous revolutionary institutions in the history of religion. It did not depend on a sacred locality or on a professional priesthood" (in H. D. Lasswell and Harland Cleveland, eds., *The Ethic of Power: The Interplay of Religion, Philosophy and Politics* [New York: Harper, 1962], pp. 3-21; see also Karl Baus, "Apostolic Community to Constantine," [New York: Herder & Herder, 1965], pp. 152-54).

Josephus cites the historian Strabo in this connection: "These Jews are already gotten into all cities, and it is hard to find a place in the habitable earth that has not admitted their tribe of men, and is not possessed by them." Josephus *Antiquities of the Jews* 14:7.2 (*The Complete Works of Flavius Josephus,* pp. 416-17). Strabo goes on to explain the role of Jews in Egyptian cities. Hence we have not only the mobility of Romans with which to contend, but the ghettos of displaced peoples who lodged within the cities of the empire. These demographic factors together with the rise of the synagogue are crucial elements in the strategy of Paul and his apostolic brethren.

[5]Mumford, *The City in History,* pp. 243-44.

[6]Tertullian *Apology* 37.

[7]See footnote in Stephen Neill, *A History of Christian Missions* (Harmondsworth, Middlesex: Penguin, 1964), p. 55.

[8]For excerpted passages from "The Rule of St. Benedict," see *Documents of the Christian Church,* ed. Henry Bettenson (New York: Oxford University Press, 1947), pp. 164-81.

[9]Kenneth Scott Latourette, A History of the Expansion of Christianity, vol. 2, *The Thousand Years of Uncertainty, A.D. 500-1500* (Grand Rapids, Mich.: Zondervan, 1970).

[10]A personal conversation in Dacca, Bangladesh, in June 1984.

[11]Herbert B. Workman, *The Evolution of the Monastic Ideal* (London: Epworth, 1913).

[12]Cited in Franklin H. Littel, *The Origins of Sectarian Protestantism* (New York: Macmillan, 1952), p. 121.

[13]I've been helped greatly by Gordon Rupp's "pattern thinking" in *Patterns of Reformation* (London: Epworth, 1969), but also by Steven E. Ozment, *The Reformation in the Cities: The Appeal of Protestantism to Sixteenth-century Germany and Switzerland* (New Haven, Conn.: Yale University Press, 1975), and Bernd Moeller, *Imperial Cities and the Reformation: Three Essays* (Durham, N.C.: Labyrinth Press, 1982).

[14]It was Lewis Hanke, in *Aristotle and the American Indians: A Study of Race Prejudice in the Modern World* (Chicago: Henry Regency, 1959), who revolutionized my thinking on the Spanish mission in the New World. See also Lewis Hanke, *All*

Mankind Is One: A Study of the Disputation Between Bartolomâe de Las Casas and Juan Ginâes de Sepâulveda in 1550 on the Intellectual and Religious Capacity of the American Indians (De Kalb: Northern Illinois University, 1974).

[15]I've already cited some of Williams's works in chapter 1. The baptism of Williams has evoked some continuing controversy. Leroy Moore, discussing "Roger Williams as an Enduring Symbol for Baptists" (*Church History* 34, March 1965), points out that if he really ever was a Baptist, he did not remain so, and instead John Clarke probably best deserves the honor of "Baptist Founder" in America. For Moore, the reason Williams is considered a Baptist is his views on religious liberty and freedom of conscience.

William R. Whitsitt has an appendix in *A Question in Baptist History: Whether the Anabaptists in England Practiced Immersion Before the Year 1641* (Louisville, Ky.: Charles T. Dearing, 1896). Whitsitt concludes that Williams was rebaptized in 1939 and that it was a clear case of believer's baptism. However, he can find no evidence to indicate that immersion was practiced until six years later, so he concludes that Williams, like Baptists today, believed in believers' baptism, but that he was probably sprinkled.

[16]See Mark A. Noll, *A History of Christianity in the United States and Canada* (Grand Rapids, Mich.: Eerdmans, 1992), pp. 136-38.

[17]H. C. G. Moule, *Charles Simeon* (Downers Grove, Ill.: InterVarsity Press, 1956).

[18]Charles Howard Hopkins, *John R. Mott, 1865-1955: A Biography* (Grand Rapids, Mich.: Eerdmans, 1979), and James F. Findlay, *Dwight L. Moody, American Evangelist, 1837-1899* (Chicago: University of Chicago Press, 1969).

[19]Georgina Battiscombe, *Shaftesbury: The Great Reformer, 1801-1885* (Boston: Houghton Mifflin, 1975).

[20]Daniel Levine, *Jane Addams and the Liberal Tradition* (Madison: State Historical Society of Wisconsin, 1971).

[21]Walter Rauschenbusch, *Christianity and the Social Crisis* (New York: Macmillan, 1913).

[22]William D. Miller, *Dorothy Day: A Biography* (San Francisco: Harper & Row, 1982).

[23]Emil Brunner, *Man in Revolt: A Christian Anthropology* (Philadelphia: Westminster, 1957). The original was published in 1937.

Chapter 26: Reflections
[1]Edward Gibbon, *Decline and Fall of the Roman Empire*, vol. 1 (New York: The Heritage Press, 1949), pp. 689-91.

[2]That is why I resonate so favorably with David Hansen's comment in his marvelous recent book on rural pastoral ministry, *The Art of Pastoring: Ministry Without All the Answers* (Downers Grove, Ill.: InterVarsity Press, 1994): "I discovered that spending a day reading thirty pages of Karl Barth's *Dogmatics* helped me more in my pastoral work than reading a hundred pages of how-to literature" (p. 10).

[3]Albert C. Outler, ed., *John Wesley* (New York: Oxford University Press, 1964).

[4]The United Nations-sponsored human-rights discussions and the 1995 women's

conference in China exposed major fault lines in East-West thinking on these issues. Islam is increasingly challenging the West culturally in France and many Western cities on these issues.

[5]Globalization has become a buzzword in theological circles. It's now a missiological reality that the emerging churches of Latin America, Africa and Asia function as a conservative theological and cultural brake on Western theological and social agendas, even while prodding the West on political and economic fronts.

[6]In Isaiah 58:1-12 the worship moves as a seamless robe into service in the streets and culminates with the rebuilding of the streets.

[7]Margaret Clarkson, "Our Cities Cry to You" (Wheaton, Ill.: Hope Music Publishing, 1987). Used by permission.